THE MAKING *of* A
SPIRITUAL
WARRIOR

THE MAKING *of* A
SPIRITUAL WARRIOR

A WOMAN'S GUIDE
TO DAILY VICTORY

QUIN SHERRER
——— AND ———
RUTHANNE GARLOCK

COMPILED BY BETH NETHERY FEIA

SERVANT PUBLICATIONS
ANN ARBOR, MICHIGAN

Vine Books is an imprint of Servant Publications especially designed to serve evangelical Christians.

All Scripture quotations, unless otherwise indicated, are taken from the HOLY BIBLE, NEW INTERNATIONAL VERSION. © 1973, 1978, 1984 by International Bible Society. Used by permission of Zondervan Publishing House. All rights reserved. Other versions are abbreviated as follows: AMPLIFIED (The Amplified Bible), KJV (King James Version), NKJV (New King James Version), LB (The Living Bible), NASB (New American Standard Bible), Phillips (New Testament in Modern English), and Weymouth.

This book has been compiled from the following sources: *How to Pray for Your Family and Friends,* © 1990; *A Woman's Guide to Spiritual Warfare,* © 1991; *The Spiritual Warrior's Prayer Guide,* © 1992; *A Woman's Guide to Breaking Bondages,* © 1994; *A Woman's Guide to Spirit-Filled Living,* © 1996; *A Woman's Guide to Getting Through Tough Times,* © 1998, all written and copyrighted by Quin Sherrer and Ruthanne Garlock. Published by Servant Publications, Box 8617, Ann Arbor, Michigan, 48107. Used with permission.

Published by Servant Publications
P.O. Box 8617
Ann Arbor, Michigan 48107

Cover design: D2 Design Works, Sisters, Oregon
Cover photograph: Tony Stone Images

02   10 9 8 7 6 5

Printed in the United States of America
ISBN 1-56955-111-1

LIBRARY OF CONGRESS CATALOGING-IN-PUBLICATION DATA

Sherrer, Quin.
　　The making of a spiritual warrior / Quin Sherrer and Ruthanne Garlock : compiled by Beth Nethery Feia.
　　　　p.   cm.
　　"Comprised of material excerpted from six of our previous titles"—Introd.
　　ISBN 1-56955-111-1 (alk. paper)
　　1. Christian women—Religious life.   2. Spiritual warfare.   I. Garlock, Ruthanne.   II. Feia, Beth.   III. Title.
BV4527.S425   1999
248.8'43—dc21

98-37328
CIP

Although of course we lead normal human lives, the battle we are fighting is on the spiritual level. The very weapons we use are not those of human warfare but powerful in God's warfare for the destruction of the enemy's strongholds. Our battle is to bring down every deceptive fantasy and every imposing defense that men erect against the true knowledge of God. We even fight to capture every thought until it acknowledges the authority of Christ.

2 CORINTHIANS 10:3-5, PHILLIPS

CONTENTS

PART I:
PREPARING FOR BATTLE

PART II:
WHEN THE BATTLE RAGES

PART III:
MARKS OF SPIRITUAL POWER

PART IV:
STANDING FIRM

SPIRITUAL LANDMINES

PRACTICING THE SPIRITUAL DISCIPLINES

INTRODUCTION

This volume is comprised of material excerpted from six of our previous titles published by Servant Publications:

A Woman's Guide to Spiritual Warfare
A Woman's Guide to Breaking Bondages
A Woman's Guide to Spirit-Filled Living
A Woman's Guide to Getting Through Tough Times
How to Pray for Your Family & Friends
The Spiritual Warrior's Prayer Guide

Over the ten years we've been writing books together, awareness of and interest in prayer and spiritual warfare has steadily increased. Some may have felt it was merely a new fad among Christians, but growing numbers of our readers have come to believe a woman's place is in the war!

Whether we like it or not, there is a war going on around us, and God has given women places in the battle. He provides potent weapons and equips us to participate in evicting the enemy from territory he's stolen from God's people. He simply wants us to cooperate with his eternal purposes.

Our goal in this handbook for spiritual warriors is to energize and instruct you for the daily struggles you face.

The book is arranged so that for three months you can use one reading a day for a meditation.

We encourage you to proclaim the message that Jesus has the power to change people and circumstances in families, neighborhoods, cities, and nations, as these verses declare:

The Lord gives the command;
The women who proclaim the good tidings are a great host:
"Kings of armies flee, they flee,
And she who remains at home will divide the spoil!"

PSALM 68:11-12, NASB

"Speech is the woman's ministry," says our friend, evangelist Dick Mills. "Verbal expression goes with a woman's calling. It was women who proclaimed the good news about the destruction of Pharoah, the death of Goliath, and the resurrection of Christ."

Yes, women, we do have a message, and we do have a part in the battle. We are counted in the host of women who can proclaim the defeat of the enemy and the victory of our Lord Jesus Christ. The Holy Spirit calls and empowers us to take up this challenge and experience spiritual breakthrough.

We pray this book will inspire and challenge you to be among the women whose hope is anchored in the unshakable power of God.

— Quin Sherrer & Ruthanne Garlock

PART ONE:

PREPARING *for* BATTLE

Put on the full armor of God so that you can take your stand against the devil's schemes. For our struggle is not against flesh and blood, but against the rulers, against the authorities, against the powers of this dark world and against the spiritual forces of evil in the heavenly realms.

EPHESIANS 6:11-12

Father, through the guidance of your Spirit, open my eyes to the schemes of the evil one that threaten me and those I love. Help me not to shrink back but to stand firm in the fight against principalities and powers.

YOU MUST FIGHT!

A friend once said to me, "Quin, I never wanted to have to fight the devil. I just wanted to remain a normal Christian, go to church, mind my own business, and not cause trouble!" But when her son got into drugs, she learned spiritual warfare out of necessity.

Thousands of women feel they've been tending to "business as usual," trying their best to live a good Christian life. Suddenly an iron chariot comes roaring through their household, church, business, or community, thrusting them into confrontation with the enemy. And they cry out, "Help!"

Satan is God's enemy, but if we are God's children, he is our enemy too. In these verses the apostle Paul warns us about the enemy. The devil and his invisible demonic forces devise plans or schemes to use against us—particularly if we seem to be a threat to his kingdom of darkness.

But God has given us his weapons, his name, his authority, the blood of Jesus, the written Word of God, praise, prayer, and the Holy Spirit's guidance.

The Holy Spirit equips us to stand firm in the midst of battles raging around us. And he teaches us how to pray.

Lead us not into temptation, but deliver us from the evil one.

MATTHEW 6:13

Be self-controlled and alert. Your enemy the devil prowls around like a roaring lion looking for someone to devour. Resist him, standing firm in the faith.

1 PETER 5:8, 9a

Satan himself masquerades as an angel of light.

2 CORINTHIANS 11:14b

Father, your Word exposes Satan and calls me to resist him by embracing truth and living fully for you. Equip me to do battle when he tries to deceive me and those around me. Be my captain in this fight. I am on your side, Lord.

OUR ADVERSARY

The name Satan actually means "adversary, or one who opposes." Any discussion about warfare with this enemy tends to repel many believers. To ignore him, however, and to hope he will ignore us is both unrealistic and hazardous.

God and Satan are not equally powerful forces standing in opposition to one another. The devil has real power, which Christians would be wise to respect. But as a created being in no way equal with God, his power is limited.

Arthur Mathews says:

The terrifying fact of a hostile world of evil and malicious spirits paralyzes many Christians into inactivity and unwillingness to seek out biblical answers and to apply them.... There are many clear indications of Satan's motives and methods given us in the Bible, if only we would heed them.... His central purpose is to pull God from His throne in the minds of men and to take that throne himself.[1]

Our goal as spiritual warriors is to see men and women set free from the bondage of Satan by the power of the blood of Jesus.

He [Satan] was a murderer from the beginning, not holding to the truth, for there is no truth in him. When he lies, he speaks his native language, for he is a liar and the father of lies.

JOHN 8:44

If our gospel is veiled, it is veiled to those who are perishing. The god of this age has blinded the minds of unbelievers, so that they cannot see the light of the gospel of the glory of Christ, who is the image of God.

2 CORINTHIANS 4:3-4

Father, your love has broken through my blindness and rescued me from the evil one. I praise you for salvation from sin and death. I stand against my adversary and his work to blind those who need to know you. Use me, Lord, to intercede for them. Use me to open their eyes to who you are.

THE ENEMY'S METHODS

"Quin, you've offended some of the women here." Rather apologetically, the leader spoke to me after the first session of a prayer workshop I was teaching for pastors' wives. "Several of them have Ph.D.'s, and they don't believe Christians need to fight the devil in our day and age. Please tone down your message."

I'd only shared basics, stating that Satan—not another person—is our enemy, and we need to be on guard against his tactics. I was stunned by their reaction.

C.S. Lewis wrote, "There are two equal and opposite errors into which our race can fall about the devils. One is to disbelieve in their existence. The other is to believe, and to feel an excessive and unhealthy interest in them."[2]

Jesus completed the work the Father gave him to do on earth, and the enemy can do nothing to change that perfect plan of salvation. But Satan *does* keep people from hearing the message; he also distorts and misrepresents the message. In other words, he vents his rage against the Father by taking vengeance on us. Satan tries to prevent our deliverance and keep us alienated from God, knowing this frustrates God's desire to see us reconciled with him.

The Lord sold them into the hands of Jabin, a king of Canaan.... Because he had nine hundred iron chariots and had cruelly oppressed the Israelites for twenty years, they cried to the Lord for help.

JUDGES 4:2a, 3

Then Deborah said to Barak, "Go! This is the day the Lord has given [the enemy] into your hands...." On that day God subdued Jabin, the Canaanite king, before the Israelites.... Then the land had peace forty years.

JUDGES 4:14, 23; 5:31b

Lord, give me the courage of Deborah to stand against the enemy's iron chariots in my life. Forgive me for trying to deal with these issues in my own wisdom. I wait upon you to receive your strategy and your strength for fighting these battles.

BECOMING A WARRIOR

The biblical Deborah challenges us to deal with the spiritual battles at hand. She was a judge and prophetess at a time when Israel was suffering bitter oppression under Jabin, a king who had defeated and occupied Israel.

She must have heard daily reports of Jabin's cruel treatment and become increasingly incensed over the situation as the people cried out to the Lord. God responded by telling Deborah to instruct Barak, general of Israel's army, to gather troops and go to Mount Tabor. He promised to lure the enemy to that place and give victory if Israel would obey him. (See Judges 4:6-7.)

Deborah staked the nation's future on God's promise and accompanied Barak in leading the troops to battle. God would not do it for them without their effort, nor did he reveal the entire strategy in advance. They had to obey God without knowing all the reasons why. But the text says, "the Lord threw the enemy into a panic, and ... not one man was left alive" (Judges 4:15-16, LB).

These same principles apply in the battles we face. The enemy's iron chariots come in all sizes! But by prayer and spiritual warfare, we modern Deborahs can take a stand against the enemy's oppression.

*He who dwells in the shelter of the Most High
will rest in the shadow of the Almighty.*

PSALM 91:1

*Finally, be strong in the Lord and in his mighty
power.*

EPHESIANS 6:10

Father, I am under your protection as long as I obey your commands. I thank you for calling me back when I stray from your will. You have provided me with all I need to resist temptation and spiritual attack. Keep me alert and strong through the power of your Spirit.

PROTECTED AND EQUIPPED

Our basic human weaknesses make us susceptible to the enemy's activity. Though God's great power far exceeds the power of Satan, we humans are no matches for the devil if we're operating in our own strength. William Gurnall, a seventeenth-century scholar, wrote this advice:

> If you are going to take shelter under this attribute [God's almighty power], you must stay within its shade. What good will the shadow of a mighty rock do if we sit in the open sun?... We are weak in ourselves; our strength lies in the rock of God's almightiness. It should be our constant habitation.[3]

Despite some Christian's exploits for God, they lose the inner contest. They walk out from under the sheltering rock of God's almighty power. Of course, the Father's mercy allows for them to be restored and healed, but how much better it is "to be made new in the attitude of your minds" (Ephesians 4:23) and to walk in mastery over these struggles.

God has provided all we need to defeat this adversary of ours—both the enemy within and the enemy without. We *can* triumph if we choose to employ God's provision and obey his instructions.

Therefore put on the complete armor of God, so that you may be able to stand your ground in the evil day, and, having fought to the end, to remain victors on the field. Stand therefore, first fastening round you the girdle of truth and putting on the breastplate of uprightness as well as the shoes of the gospel of peace—a firm foundation for your feet. And besides all these take the great shield of faith, on which you will be able to quench all the flaming darts of the Wicked One; and receive the helmet of salvation, and the sword of the Spirit which is the word of God. Pray with unceasing prayer and entreaty at all times in the Spirit, and be always on the alert to seize opportunities for doing so.

EPHESIANS 6:13-18, WEYMOUTH

Father, thank you for giving me spiritual armor that protects me from the enemy and equips me to fight. It's one thing to know I have these weapons but quite another to remember them in times of attack. Train me, Lord, so I can effectively use what you have given me.

YOUR SPIRITUAL WARDROBE

These verses are Paul's battle handbook for the churches he had founded. He wanted to prepare them for the persecution and other adversity he knew would come. His writings are still the "basic training" passages for our own spiritual conflicts today.

Only a fool would race into battle without adequate defense. A Christian likewise needs armor to provide protection against the evil one. When Paul wrote this passage he was being held under house arrest, guarded by Roman soldiers. The Holy Spirit inspired the analogy of the believer as a soldier in God's spiritual army.

William Gurnall wrote:

It is not left to everyone's fancy to bring whatever weapons he pleases; this would only breed chaos.... Look closely at the label to see whether the armour you wear is the workmanship of God or not. There are many imitations on the market nowadays.... Do not dare to call anything the armour of God which does not glorify him and defend you against the power of Satan![4]

The armor God provides is for our *defense* against evil powers. He also provides *offensive* weapons. Our warfare wardrobe is complete in every detail, but it is our responsibility to put it on and to use it.

Although they claimed to be wise, they became fools and exchanged the glory of the immortal God for images.... Therefore God gave them over in the sinful desires of their hearts.... They exchanged the truth of God for a lie, and worshiped and served created things rather than the Creator.

ROMANS 1:22-25

But we ought always to thank God for you, brothers loved by the Lord, because from the beginning God chose you to be saved through the sanctifying work of the Spirit and through belief in the truth.... Stand firm and hold to the teachings we passed on to you.

2 THESSALONIANS 2:13, 15

Father, I love your truth. It gives me life and hope. I treasure your Word in my heart and meditate on your truth. May I be eager to believe and ready to hold fast in all circumstances to what you have revealed to me.

BELT OF TRUTH

The girdle to which Paul refers in Ephesians was actually a wide metal or leather belt worn by a soldier around his lower torso to hold his armor tightly against his body and to support his sword. It was also used to carry money and other valuables. To "gird on your sword" was to prepare for action. (See 1 Samuel 25:13, KJV.)

Satan first assaulted the truth in the garden when he asked Eve, "Did God really say…?" (Genesis 3:1b). Not having the belt of truth for armor, she wavered and began to doubt what God had said. Our enemy still uses this subtle weapon of doubt against us.

Because of the predisposition to sin with which we are born, all of us are easy prey for deception if our spiritual armor is not firmly in place. We can be deceived by the devil or his emissaries, by the seduction and smooth talk of others, by our own pride, or our selfishness or greed.

The truth is the very essence of the gospel: God's plan to free us from sin's bondage through his Son's sacrificial death, burial, and resurrection. It is the crux of every battle we face. We must fasten it on tightly to protect us from the strategies of the evil one.

The mind of sinful man is death, but the mind controlled by the Spirit is life and peace.... You ... are controlled not by the sinful nature but by the Spirit, if the Spirit of God lives in you.... If Christ is in you, your body is dead because of sin, yet your spirit is alive because of righteousness.

ROMANS 8:6, 9-10

Let us put aside the deeds of darkness and put on the armor of light.... Clothe yourselves with the Lord Jesus Christ, and do not think about how to gratify the desires of the sinful nature.

ROMANS 13:12b, 14

Father, I am often tempted to compromise when doing what is right proves difficult or dangerous, but sinning never provides the escape and ease that I seek. Give me greater conviction to hold to what is right and true. Strengthen me to flee from temptation. Your righteousness is my protection.

BREASTPLATE OF RIGHTEOUSNESS

This piece of armor (today's equivalent is the bullet-proof vest) protects the heart and other vital organs of the soldier. The girdle or belt of truth holds it in place. *Righteousness* simply means "right action," "uprightness," or "conformity to the will of God."[5] It is important to remember that truth and righteousness always go together.

"Keep and guard your heart with all vigilance ... for out of it flow the springs of life," advised Solomon (Proverbs 4:23, AMPLIFIED). Satan often tempts us to compromise our standard of righteousness with the argument, "But it's for a good cause."

Gurnall writes:

Head knowledge of the things of Christ is not enough; this following Christ is primarily a matter of the heart.... If you are a serious soldier, do not flirt with any of your desires that are beneath Christ and heaven. They will play the harlot and steal your heart.[6]

Righteousness and holiness are God's protection to defend the believer's conscience from all wounds inflicted by sin.... Your holiness is what the devil wants to steal from you.... He will allow a man to have anything, or be anything, rather than be truly and powerfully holy.[7]

Great peace have they who love your law, and nothing can make them stumble.

PSALM 119:165

Live a life worthy of the calling you have received.... Make every effort to keep the unity of the Spirit through the bond of peace.

EPHESIANS 4:1b, 3

Father, only the supernatural peace you give is lasting. I choose to surrender my fears to you and put on your peace. Empower me by your Holy Spirit to walk in unity with others and radiate your peace wherever I go.

SHOES OF PEACE

The shoes of peace symbolize readiness. When a soldier put on his shoes, it meant he was preparing to report for duty and face the enemy. The soldier's shoes protected his feet and sometimes were fitted with metal cleats to make him more sure-footed in combat. God told his people to eat the Passover meal with their shoes on so they would be ready to flee from Egypt. (See Exodus 12:11.)

As Christian soldiers we wear our shoes of peace to invade enemy territory, bearing the Good News and reconciling man with God. "He has committed to us the message of reconciliation" (2 Corinthians 5:19).

Again we share Gurnall's wisdom:

The peace which the gospel brings to the heart makes a saint ready to wade through any trouble that might meet him in his Christian course.... Only Christ can make a shoe fit the Christian's foot so he can easily walk a hard path, because He lines it with the peace of the gospel.... The most important provision Christ made for His disciples was not to leave them a quiet world to live in, but to arm them against a volatile and troublesome world.[8]

But the righteousness that is by faith says: "… The word is near you; it is in your mouth and in your heart," that is, the word of faith we are proclaiming: That if you confess with your mouth, "Jesus is Lord," and believe in your heart that God has raised him from the dead, you will be saved…. As the Scripture says, "Anyone who trusts in him will never be put to shame."

ROMANS 10:6-11

The Lord is my strength and my shield; my heart trusts in him, and I am helped.

PSALM 28:7

Thank you, Father, for the shield of faith that enables me to deflect the enemy's flaming arrows. The steadfastness of your character assures me that I can place my trust in you. Help me to use this piece of armor effectively in the midst of battle.

SHIELD OF FAITH

Various kinds of shields were used in Paul's day, but the metaphor in Ephesians 6:16 refers to the large rectangular shield that could protect the entire body. It was common practice for the soldier to anoint his shield with oil so it would reflect the sun's rays and blind the enemy, as well as deflect his blows. Gurnall gives this insight concerning the shield:

> The apostle compares faith to a shield because ... the shield is intended for the defense of the whole body.... And if the shield was not large enough to cover every part at once, the skillful soldier could turn it this way or that way, to stop the swords or the arrows, no matter where they were directed.... Not only does the shield defend the whole body, but it defends the soldier's other armour also.... Every grace derives its safety from faith; each one lies secure under the shadow of faith.[9]

Our confidence in God must be based on his character and trustworthiness, not on our own ability to follow a formula. Simply put, faith means believing that God is who he says he is and that he will do what he says he will do.

33

The weapons we fight with are not the weapons of the world. On the contrary, they have divine power to demolish strongholds. We demolish arguments and every pretension that sets itself up against the knowledge of God, and we take captive every thought to make it obedient to Christ.

2 CORINTHIANS 10:4-5

But since we belong to the day, let us be self-controlled, putting on faith and love as a breastplate, and the hope of salvation as a helmet.

1 THESSALONIANS 5:8

Father, you know my thoughts and the battles I often wage in my mind. Without the renewing power of your Spirit, my mind is a breeding ground for sin. I place the helmet of salvation on my head. Help me to think thoughts that are pleasing to you, and banish from my mind all thoughts of doubt, fear, and unbelief.

HELMET OF SALVATION

The hope of salvation protects the Christian against attacks on his mind, one of Satan's primary targets. To deal with such an attack we must learn to distinguish the voice of our enemy from God's voice. God will speak words of love, comfort, conviction, and guidance. The enemy speaks words of fear, accusation, and condemnation.

Dean Sherman's analogy is helpful:

Every military post has guards. They stand quietly at their posts until they hear a rustling in the bushes. Then they immediately ask, "Who goes there?" and are prepared to evict any intruder. We too need to post a guard at the gate of our minds to check the credentials of every thought and every imagination, ready to cast down that which is not true, not righteous, or not of God. If it doesn't belong, out it goes. This is spiritual warfare: being alert to every thought.[10]

Our renewed minds should profoundly influence our behavior so those in the world recognize we are Christians in both word and in deed. Keeping our minds renewed in Christ also protects us from deception.

Author Roger Palms writes, "Think of life as a hard-hat area. Think of the hope of salvation as a helmet. It will change your perspective on how you face each day and the events in it."[11]

Jesus answered, "It is written: 'Man does not live on bread alone, but on every word that comes from the mouth of God.'"

MATTHEW 4:4

For the word of God is living and active. Sharper than any double-edged sword, it penetrates even to dividing soul and spirit, joints and marrow; it judges the thoughts and attitudes of the heart.

HEBREWS 4:12

Father, I love your Word and long to obey it. Make it come alive to me so that I can competently use this powerful sword against the enemy. Help me treasure your Word in my heart so I might not sin against you.

SWORD OF THE SPIRIT

The sword of the Spirit is used for both defense and offense. The better we know the Word of God, the more adept we will be at wielding this weapon to oppose the powers of evil. The Word is not only a spiritual weapon; it is a source of great comfort.

Arthur Mathews challenges us:

If we accept the fact that our role in life is that of soldiers, then we must drop our toys and become more acquainted with the weapons of our warfare. In a conflict situation a soldier's best friend is his weapon, because it is his one resource for disposing of the enemy, securing his own safety, and accomplishing the will of his captain.

… Unused weapons do not inflict casualties on the enemy nor win wars…. It is not enough to give mental assent to the fact that a spiritual warfare is going on. Passivity towards our enemy is what the devil wants from us and is his trick to cool the ardor of God's men of war.[12]

Then he quotes missionary Amy Carmichael: "The only thing that matters is to throw all the energies of our being into the faithful use of this precious blade. Then, and only then, may we rest our cause upon His Holy Word."[13]

The seventy-two returned with joy, and said, "Lord, even the demons submit to us in your name." He replied, "... I have given you authority to trample on snakes and scorpions and to overcome all the power of the enemy; nothing will harm you."

LUKE 10:17-19

God exalted him to the highest place and gave him the name that is above every name, that at the name of Jesus every knee should bow.

PHILIPPIANS 2:9, 10a

They overcame him [Satan] by the blood of the Lamb and by the word of their testimony.

REVELATION 12:11

Father, I cannot thank you enough for Jesus—his salvation, his intercession, and the power in his name! I praise you for exalting the name of your Son above every other name.

THE NAME OF JESUS

The only way to use the name of Jesus as a weapon is to speak to the enemy. Jesus spoke to Satan in the wilderness. (See Luke 4:4, 8, 12.) He also spoke to a fig tree and cursed it. (See Matthew 21:19.) So don't feel reticent about speaking to the evil powers of darkness. Paul Billheimer encourages us in this confrontation:

Many believers have been so tyrannized and dominated by Satan and the prevailing theology of Satan's power and invincibility that, like me, they would never dare to speak directly to him, even in the name of Jesus. For years, I couldn't imagine Satan running away.... When I mustered enough courage to speak directly to him in the name of Jesus, it was a great surprise to me to discover an immediate sense of deliverance—as though he had vanished, melted away.

... The only way we can be sure that he knows we are resisting him is to *speak aloud,* to directly and audibly confront him with the truth.

May I remind you again that *our resistance* by itself is not what causes Satan to flee; he flees because of the *power of Jesus* which is ours through prayer.[14]

When He, the Spirit of truth, has come, He will guide you into all truth.... Whatever He hears He will speak; and He will tell you things to come.

JOHN 16:13, NKJV

Stand fast therefore in the liberty by which Christ has made us free.... If we live in the Spirit, let us also walk in the Spirit.

GALATIANS 5:1, 25, NKJV

Father, I have often failed to consult you in decisions or to wait for your guidance. I want to walk in the Spirit much more consistently. Teach me how to listen to and obey your direction.

LET THE SPIRIT GUIDE YOU

What does it mean to walk in the Spirit? David Wilkerson, pastor of Times Square Church in New York City, has expressed it well:

> Walking in the Spirit means incredible, detailed direction and unclouded decisions. The Holy Ghost provides absolute, clearly detailed instructions to those who walk in Him. If you walk in the Spirit, then you don't walk in confusion—your decisions aren't clouded ones.
>
> The early Christians did not walk in confusion. They were led by the Spirit in every decision, every move, every action! The Spirit talked to them and directed them in their every waking hour. No decision was made without consulting Him. The church's motto throughout the New Testament was "He who has ears to hear, let him hear what the Spirit has to say." … Give much quality time to communion with the Holy Spirit. He will *not* speak to anyone who is in a hurry. All of God's Word is about waiting on Him.[15]

If we want to walk in the Spirit, we will learn to know his voice with distinct precision. We will listen for his direction and be willing to spend whatever time it takes in his presence. Walking in the Spirit is an adventure you won't want to miss!

I am your servant; give me discernment.

PSALM 119:125a

This my prayer: that your love may abound more and more in knowledge and depth of insight, so that you may be able to discern what is best and may be pure and blameless until the day of Christ.

PHILIPPIANS 1:9-10

Father, help me to discern your voice. If the impression I have comes from your Holy Spirit, I pray you will cause it to become more clear. If you want me to take specific action, increase my urge to act. But if this idea is not from you, please cause it to fade. Lord, I want you to be glorified in my life.

DEVELOP SPIRITUAL
DISCERNMENT

Ever since the Garden of Eden, women have had to guard against deception. The crafty devil will whisper in our ears as he did in Eve's, "Indeed, has God said... ?"

We need a radar system that flashes, "WARNING! Enemy at work." As we ask God for direction and await his response, we must discern between three possible voices: our own, God's, or Satan's.

We produce the majority of our thoughts ourselves. For example, we make plans for our families and ourselves, think through solutions to problems, and draw conclusions based on our knowledge of a situation. But often our knowledge is incomplete, our thinking flawed, and thus we're susceptible to error and deception.

Our thoughts can also come from God. The Creator can speak into our minds with a spark of revelation or an inner voice, by the gift of a word of knowledge, through Scripture verses, songs, sermons, or devotional readings. God can speak in any way he chooses.

The third possible source of a thought is our enemy. Satan and his representatives seek to influence us by planting in our minds thoughts that are contrary to God's Word or purpose. The instant you recognize the enemy's voice, immediately resist him and silence him.

Then Samuel said, "Speak, for your servant is listening."

1 SAMUEL 3:10

While they were worshiping the Lord and fasting, the Holy Spirit said, "Set apart for me Barnabas and Saul for the work for which I have called them."

ACTS 13:2

Father, I eagerly desire to practice the discipline of listening to your voice. As I worship and wait before you, speak through your Holy Spirit. I long for you to reveal the work to which you are calling me.

LISTEN WHEN GOD SPEAKS

In her book *The Mighty Warrior*, Elizabeth Alves gives these guidelines to hearing the voice of God:

- Bind the voice of the enemy.
- Submit your own will and reasoning to the Holy Spirit.
- Turn off your own problems.
- Give your undivided attention to God's Word.
- Limit your own talking.
- Write it down. (The Spirit of the Lord will speak to you through impressions or pictures in the theater of your mind. When this happens, write them down.)
- Don't argue mentally.
- Wait upon the Lord for the interpretation.
- Don't get ahead of or lag behind the Holy Spirit.
- The Holy Spirit sometimes speaks through music. Listen.
- Pay attention to your dreams. Write them down. Not all dreams are of God.
- Don't be afraid of silence. Don't be upset if you don't hear anything when you pray. The Holy Spirit may just want you to worship the Lord.[16]

God is a loving Father. When we pray and ask him for guidance, we can be certain of two things:

1. His answer or direction to us will not be contrary to his Word as recorded in the Bible.
2. It will not be contrary to his character.

Dear friends, do not believe every spirit, but test the spirits to see whether they are from God, because many false prophets have gone out into the world. This is how you recognize the Spirit of God: Every spirit that acknowledges that Jesus Christ has come in the flesh is from God, but every spirit that does not acknowledge Jesus is not from God. This is the spirit of the antichrist.

1 JOHN 4:1-3a

Jesus himself warned his followers: "Watch out that you are not deceived."

LUKE 21:8a

Father, help me to rebuke Satan and to command him to be silent when he tries to influence my thoughts. Thank you for giving me authority over him through the blood of Jesus.

TEST THE SPIRITS

Once when I (Ruthanne) was praying for a loved one, I suddenly recognized the voice of the enemy. "What makes you think praying will help?" the voice taunted. "He'll never change!"

For a moment I abruptly stopped praying. Then I addressed the enemy: "Satan, I command you to be silent. You have no authority to speak to me. I resist you and refuse to hear your voice, in Jesus' name. I declare that I have the mind of Christ (see 1 Corinthians 2:16) and that my prayer is according to the will of God."

Bible teacher Dean Sherman explains:

When the Scriptures speak of Satan or the devil, sometimes they are referring to his evil empire rather than the individual, Lucifer himself. The devil couldn't possibly be in hundreds of thousands of places at the same time, tempting people and putting suggestions in their minds. His fallen angels are the ones carrying out Satan's orders.... When God's Word tells us to resist the devil, I believe it is telling us to resist spirit beings belonging to Lucifer.

... While the forces of darkness cannot read our minds—only God can do that (Psalm 7:9)—they can put suggestions there.... Most spiritual warfare takes place in the human mind.[17]

He calls his own sheep by name and leads them out.
When he has brought out all his own, he goes on
ahead of them, and his sheep follow him because
they know his voice. But they will never follow a
stranger; in fact, they will run away from him
because they do not recognize a stranger's voice.

JOHN 10:3b-5

Father, I need a fresh anointing of discernment. Along
with discernment, I ask for wisdom, understanding, and
knowledge. Let me learn to distinguish your voice from all
the other voices vying for my attention. May your sweet
Holy Spirit be so real to me that I will yield to his direction
and guidance.

STAY CLOSE TO THE SHEPHERD

For many believers, the idea of asking God for guidance, then discerning his response, is a scary proposition. They don't feel capable of hearing from God. Isn't it only super-spiritual people who can do that?

That's exactly what the enemy wants you to think. It keeps you from doing damage to his territory. Or it keeps you running from place to place, hoping to "get a word from God" through someone else.

Any person willing to spend the necessary time in worship, prayer, meditation, and Bible reading can hear from God. He is our shepherd, and he gives us his promise.

We learn to recognize God's voice by staying close to him, as a sheep stays close to his shepherd. If you're a wounded sheep, you stay especially close and allow him to heal you. Now and then the shepherd may even carry you for a while, but he can't do that if you run away. The closer you are to the shepherd, the more familiar his voice becomes and the more you prefer it above the noise of the world.

Recognizing the voice of an imposter is not so difficult when you truly know your shepherd's voice.

Do not be anxious about anything, but in everything, by prayer and petition, with thanksgiving, present your requests to God.

PHILIPPIANS 4:6

If our hearts do not condemn us, we have confidence before God and receive from him anything we ask, because we obey his commands and do what pleases him.

1 JOHN 3:21-22

Thank you, Lord, for the wonderful privilege of prayer. Help me to be more diligent to pray as you direct, knowing that I am praying according to your will. Thank you for your promise that you hear us.

THE POWER OF PRAYER

"Lord, I've looked everywhere for the keys, and I can't find them," the eight-year-old boy prayed desperately. "Please forgive me for playing with Dad's car keys. I know I shouldn't have. But now I'm going from this spot at my friend's house straight to my room, and I'm asking you please to have those keys lying on top of the bureau when I get there. In Jesus' name, Amen."

This petition was prayed years ago by Ruthanne's husband when he lived with his parents on a mission station in West Africa. After praying he left the neighbor's house where he'd been searching and cut across the yard, the most direct route to his bedroom. As he went he tripped on something in the tall grass—the lost keys!

God answered but not according to the boy's instructions. In the process he learned a lesson we all need to learn: God does answer prayer, but he does it in his own way and by his own timetable.

We sometimes presume we know how to pray for people or situations, telling God what to do about it. How important it is to listen to God's directions for prayer and then follow the Holy Spirit's leading. Thankfully, God looks on our hearts, and his mercy covers our mistakes.

He [the Lord] saw that there was no one, he was appalled that there was no one to intervene.

ISAIAH 59:16a

I looked for a man among them who would build up the wall and stand before me in the gap on behalf of the land so I would not have to destroy it, but I found none.

EZEKIEL 22:30

Therefore he is able to save completely those who come to God through him, because he always lives to intercede for them.

HEBREWS 7:25

Father, give me a heart for those around me who are in need. Teach me how to intercede on their behalf, doing battle for them in prayer. I think of your Son, who faithfully intercedes day and night on my behalf, who never forgets my needs. Help me to become more like him.

INTERCESSION IS
INTERVENTION

"Without God, we cannot. Without us, God will not." St. Augustine's succinct statement sums up the twofold nature of intercession.

God empowers us by the Holy Spirit to intercede for others' needs; without that empowerment our prayers would be empty words. He also invests us with Christ's authority to restrain satanic forces that are blinding and hindering the person for whom we're praying.

When we intercede for the needs of another, we stand between God and that person, beseeching God on his or her behalf. We also stand, however, between that person and Satan, doing spiritual battle. It therefore seems accurate to say that *intercession* is *intervention.*

Of course, Jesus is the ultimate intercessor, the one who stands in the gap between God and man. He became the perfect mediator by giving himself as a sacrifice for sin. He equips us and commissions us to intercede by pushing back the enemy, thus allowing the Holy Spirit to bring conviction that leads to repentance.

You can pray for your family members while you make beds, wash clothes, vacuum the house, prepare meals, mow the lawn, or take your turn driving in the carpool. You can pray on the way to work, in elevators, while waiting for appointments, or in supermarket checkout lines.

Pray in the Spirit on all occasions with all kinds of prayers and requests. With this in mind, be alert and always keep on praying for all the saints.

EPHESIANS 6:18

I will pray with my spirit, but I will also pray with my mind.

1 CORINTHIANS 14:15

Father, help me to become more sensitive to your inner prompting to bear the burdens of others and intercede for them. Reveal to me how you want me to pray. Find in me a willing intercessor both day and night.

PRAY IN THE SPIRIT

Many women have told us of times when the Holy Spirit alerted them to pray for someone they didn't know: a person they had seen only in passing, a total stranger, or a public figure or celebrity. It may be a long-term prayer assignment or a one-time call to prayer for the moment.

Kerry shared with us her own such experience:

"Once I awoke in the middle of the night and prayed in tongues for what seemed like a long time. I knew my prayer language was being used to war in the heavens for something I didn't understand.

"After the prayer I asked the Lord, 'What was that all about?' He showed me the face of a man I scarcely knew, except that I'd seen him leading singing in a Sunday school class.

"'Why me, Lord?' I asked again. I felt the Lord's answer was sufficient when he impressed this thought on my heart: 'Because he is in danger, and you are the only person who is willing to wake right now and do warfare on his behalf.' We don't always know the outcome of such prayers, but I have since been willing to pray night or day for anyone God impresses upon me by the Spirit."

But you, beloved, building yourselves up on your most holy faith, praying in the Holy Spirit, keep yourselves in the love of God.

JUDE 20-21a, NKJV

He who speaks in a tongue edifies himself.

1 CORINTHIANS 14:4a

Father, help me to be conscious that when I don't know how to pray, you allow the Holy Spirit to pray through me. Help me be more alert to your still, small voice calling me to prayer. I want to be more cooperative and yielded! Thank you that this gift of praying in the Spirit also will strengthen me. I'm so grateful that you loved me enough to send your Holy Spirit.

TONGUES EDIFY US

Praying in tongues is a way to build up or strengthen your own faith. In other words, praying in the Spirit is not only a means of intercession for others but a means of receiving strength from the Holy Spirit ourselves.

Pastor Ted Haggard says,

"Times of prayer are always dominated by something—our self-pity, our sin, our family needs or need for money, or His Spirit and His kingdom. The primary way to turn away from our own interests and become absorbed by His is to pray in the Spirit.... I find that as I pray in tongues, my priorities and thoughts are sharpened. My attitudes change, my inner man is strengthened, my faith is increased, and God drops fresh ideas into my mind."[18]

Corrie ten Boom wrote this about a missionary in China who had to endure brainwashing: "He resisted and fought against it, but the moment came when he felt he was at the end of his strength. Then he started to pray in tongues. That fellowship with the Lord ... was his salvation. The enemy could not influence his mind any longer.... It is a strong weapon and will prove to be so in the final battle."[19]

I say to you, Ask and keep on asking and it shall be given you; seek and keep on seeking and you shall find; knock and keep on knocking and the door shall be opened to you. For everyone who asks and keeps on asking receives, and he who seeks and keeps on seeking finds; and to him who knocks and keeps on knocking, the door shall be opened.

LUKE 11:9-10, AMPLIFIED

Father, I pray that *(name of individual)* be delivered from spiritual blindness and from every scheme and snare the devil has used to hold (him/her) captive. Let every stronghold of unbelief in (his/her) life be pulled down and brought into captivity to the obedience of Christ. Father, please speak to (him/her) by the Holy Spirit, revealing to (him/her) that (he/she) must call upon you to be saved—and give (him/her) the desire to do it. Lord of the harvest, send laborers across (his/her) path to share the gospel and speak into (his/her) life, and prepare (his/her) heart to receive their words.

BE BOLD AND PERSISTENT

Jesus himself tells a parable illustrating tenacious prayer. (See Luke 11.) A man has an unexpected guest. Having nothing to feed his guest, the man goes at midnight to his friend's door and persistently knocks as he asks for three loaves of bread. He knocks and knocks until he gets what he came for.

Notice how specific he was, asking for exactly what he needed: three loaves of bread. And this is not about annoying God until we get what we want, nor is it about overcoming God's reluctance. Pastor Jack Hayford writes of this parable:

> Jesus is saying, "Your first barrier isn't God—it's your own hesitancy to ask freely. You need to learn the kind of boldness that isn't afraid to ask—whatever the need or the circumstances.
>
> "... Ask with unabashed forwardness; ask with shameless boldness," he commands. "And when you do," he clearly teaches, "Your friend, my Father, will rise to the occasion and see that everything you need is provided."[20]

We encourage you to become persistent in your praying. Be open to the Holy Spirit's leading to add ideas as you pray. Your prayer is not rote repetition, nor a mechanical exercise. The flow of the Holy Spirit will keep your praying fresh.

Two are better than one, because they have a good return for their work: If one falls down, his friend can help him up.

ECCLESIASTES 4:9-10

If two of you on earth agree about anything you ask for, it will be done for you by my Father in heaven. For where two or three come together in my name, there am I with them.

MATTHEW 18:19, 20

Father, lead me to prayer partners with whom I can stand in solidarity. Bring us together through the working of your Spirit. I watch and wait for them.

PRAY TOGETHER

The prayer of agreement can be a powerful strategy in spiritual warfare.

We find it essential to have at least one specific friend—someone familiar with the current battles we're dealing with—to stand in agreement with us as prayer support. Such partners also provide a blanket of prayer for us when we're traveling, ministering—or writing a book!

Prayer partners play a spiritual role that is analogous to the army specialists who create a "corridor of safety" for the tanks and armaments to mount an offensive against the enemy. These soldiers learn to detonate land mines, clear barbed-wire entanglements, bulldoze man-made barriers, and build emergency bridges over trenches. Only then can the army invade enemy territory and liberate the captives. Prayer partners often pray in advance to help clear the way, neutralizing the enemy's offensive forces.

Individual prayer and warfare is important, but interceding with a prayer partner or a group of believers strengthens the prayer's effectiveness. If the two of you or all in the group are fasting in unity, the warfare is even stronger.

First we should ask the Lord *how* he wants us to pray. Then in agreement, *with one mind,* we pray as he directs, persisting with our prayer partners until we see results.

So is my word that goes out from my mouth: It will not return to me empty, but will accomplish what I desire and achieve the purpose for which I sent it.

ISAIAH 55:11

For the word of God is living and active. Sharper than any double-edged sword, it penetrates even to dividing soul and spirit, joints and marrow; it judges the thoughts and attitudes of the heart.

HEBREWS 4:12

Father, I want to hide your Word in my heart, to build a treasure store of your truth in my mind so that I can pray according to your Word and do battle with the Sword of your Spirit.

PRAY THE SCRIPTURE

One way to battle in prayer is to use verses of Scripture that fit the situation. Examples are Psalm 91, which could be for protection, and Psalms 140 and 141, which could be paraphrased with names of family members or friends who are being attacked by evil forces.

Here are some ways to use Scriptures both as a prayer and as warfare against the devil:

Prayer: "God ... grant to (name of person) repentance leading to knowledge of the truth, that (he/she) may come to (his/her) senses and escape from the snare of the devil, having been held captive by him to do his will." (See Luke 15:17-20; 2 Timothy 2:25b-26 NASB.)

Warfare: "Satan, you have held (name) captive to do your will, as the Word of God reveals. In the name and authority of Jesus Christ of Nazareth, loose (his/her) will so (he/she) will be free to accept Jesus as Lord and Savior." (See 2 Timothy 2:26, NASB.)

Prayer: "Lord, I pray that you will open their eyes and turn them from darkness to light, and from the power of Satan to God, so that they may receive forgiveness of sins and a place among those who are sanctified by faith in Christ." (See Acts 26:l8, NASB.)

PART TWO:

WHEN *the* BATTLE RAGES

The Lord is my shepherd, I shall not be in want.... Even though I walk through the valley of the shadow of death, I will fear no evil, for you are with me; your rod and your staff, they comfort me.

PSALM 23:1, 4

Praise be to the God and Father of our Lord Jesus Christ, the Father of compassion and the God of all comfort, who comforts us in all our troubles.

2 CORINTHIANS 1:3-4

Father, you are near to the brokenhearted, and you save those crushed in spirit. You will comfort and rescue me. You will restore me in your perfect time. I stand against the enemy's efforts to make me despair and become bitter. May none of this suffering go to waste, but may I grow in perseverance, character, and hope for the glory of your name.

WHEN YOU ARE
GRIEF-STRICKEN

In times of heartache you can know that Jesus identifies with you for he was "a man of sorrows, and familiar with suffering" (Isaiah 53:3). You are not alone. God has not failed you. He sees the end from the beginning—a much larger picture than you are able to comprehend.

Lavelda is a friend whose sixty-year-old husband, Paul, seemed quite healthy. One week he began suffering unusually severe headaches, and within a few days a brain aneurysm took his life.

"I have to believe that I'll be okay, and God will still keep me in his peace and love, even though my love of forty-two years has just gone home to Jesus," she wrote. "Over the years I've learned my circumstances are not a measuring stick for God's love. Going through tough times does not mean God doesn't love me as much as he loves someone else.

"Once I got past wondering if God was mad at me, I could receive comfort from his Word. I had to decide to believe that he meant just what he said, and refuse to be robbed by doubt. Now I realize he loves me as much as I will allow him to in any circumstance."

I will give you the treasures of darkness, riches stored in secret places, so that you may know that I am the Lord, the God of Israel, who summons you by name.

ISAIAH 45:3

Father, I often respond to hardship with complaining, frustration, discouragement, and sometimes even despair. I am impatient for you to act and resentful when I must endure. Forgive me for resisting the shaping of my character during difficult times. Show me how to find your treasures in the darkness.

HOW TO FIND
TREASURES OF DARKNESS

During a difficult period in my life years ago, I (Ruthanne) developed the habit of walking a mile every day to talk to the Lord and settle my thoughts. On my walk one crisp October morning, the Lord spoke to me through Isaiah 45:3. He said very clearly, "Ruthanne, these are precious days. I am teaching you the treasures of darkness."

He said he was teaching me as I allowed him to; there was value in the experience. I remembered reading of Jesus, "Although he was a son, he learned obedience from what he suffered" (Hebrews 5:8).

After that morning with the Lord under the trees, my circumstances actually got worse, not better. I began to see, however, that from God's point of view, my response to the difficulties was more important than the problems themselves. He obviously wanted to change me, and I finally consented.

The glory of it all for me was not just seeing circumstances change, which they eventually did. The greater blessing was that I came to know God and his character in a way only adversity can teach. I've come to believe that God does his best work in darkness: in creation, the incarnation, the Garden of Gethsemane, at Calvary—and in my own "dark night of the soul."

Heartache crushes the spirit…. A crushed spirit dries up the bones.

PROVERBS 15:13; 17:22

And the God of all grace, who called you to his eternal glory in Christ, after you have suffered a little while, will himself restore you and make you strong, firm, and steadfast.

1 PETER 5:10

Father, bind up my broken heart. Turn my mourning into dancing. Give me a garment of praise instead of a spirit of despair. I put my security and my future into your hands.

MOVING THROUGH THE GRIEF PROCESS

Grief serves as an escape valve for our emotions. It is like a teakettle's valve that allows steam to escape. It helps us acknowledge the loss, resolve the pain, and then move forward. But grief becomes a bondage for those who don't find God's help in seeking release.

Emily has been a widow now for more than twenty years, and God has been a faithful husband to her as she presses closer and closer to him. She says, "I don't look back, because if I did I would not accomplish what God has for me to do for him today." What she does for him is head up the intercessory group at her large urban church. Her advice for other widows:

Don't let bitterness, anger, or grief rob you of a fulfilled life today. Release those feelings to God.

Thank God for the spouse you had and for the good years you enjoyed together. Be grateful.

Trust the Lord to meet your needs in the areas where you once depended on a husband.

Read the Word of God, study it, and get to know the Lord personally.

Reach out to others, especially to other widows, and help bring healing into their lives.

What a wonderful God we have—he is the Father of our Lord Jesus Christ, the source of every mercy, and the one who so wonderfully comforts and strengthens us in our hardships and trials. And why does he do this? So that when others are troubled, needing our sympathy and encouragement, we can pass on to them this same help and comfort God has given us.

2 CORINTHIANS 1:3-4, LB

Father, I know that all things, even the great losses I have experienced, will work together for good because I love you. I surrender my grief to you and hold tightly to your promises. Nothing can thwart your plan for my life. You will redeem me from the pit and crown me with your lovingkindness and compassion.

HOLDING ON TO HOPE

Whether your grief stems from a divorce, the death of a loved one, a broken relationship, or some other disappointment, it's important that you not get stuck in this grief through denial, depression, or blaming. Don't allow the rest of your life to be defined by the loss you've suffered.

The enemy will do everything he can to prey on your grief and keep you bound to it. But we Christians need not grieve without hope, as unbelievers do. (See 1 Thessalonians 4:13.) In our trial of grief, we still have hope because we have access to the promises of God and his comfort.

Hannah Whitall Smith offers this antidote to fear:

A large part of the pain of life comes from the haunting "fear of evil" which so often besets us. Our lives are full of supposes. Suppose this should happen, or suppose that should happen;... how could we bear it? But, if we are living in the "high tower" of the dwelling place of God, all these supposes will drop out of our lives.... Even when walking through the valley of the shadow of death, the psalmist could say, "I will fear no evil." If we are dwelling in God, we can say so too.[21]

The one who calls you is faithful and he will do it.

1 THESSALONIANS 5:24

"For my thoughts are not your thoughts, neither are your ways my ways," declares the Lord. "As the heavens are higher than the earth, so are my ways higher than your ways and my thoughts than your thoughts."

ISAIAH 55:8-9

Father, your timing and ways are mysterious to me, but I bow before your sovereignty and trust your perfect will. Father, you are always faithful, answering my prayers in a way that is best for me in your perfect timing. I turn from insisting on my agenda. I trust in your wisdom. I wait with hope for you.

SURRENDER TO GOD'S TIMING

You've heard the saying *God is never early and he is never late*. We are the ones who get impatient and insist on our own willful timetable.

God does intervene but not always as we anticipate. Rather, he chooses to move in unexpected and surprising ways. Usually he's been preparing us all along for his divine intervention.

The Bible is full of stories about God's intervention in the lives of his handmaidens as he brought about his plan in the fullness of his timing. Consider these biblical women who experienced God's intervention:

- Hannah cried out to God, and had her barren womb healed for her Samuel to be born. (See 1 Samuel l:1-2.)
- Elizabeth, old beyond childbearing age, gave birth to John the Baptist. (See Luke 1:1-25.)
- Faithful old Anna praying in the temple was granted her desire to see the Messiah before her death. (See Luke 2:36-38.)
- A woman bent over for eighteen years was healed when Jesus put his hands on her. (See Luke 13:10-17.)
- The widow of Zarephath experienced a multiplication miracle as God replenished her small supply of flour and oil. (See 1 Kings 17:8-24.)
- Esther, Deborah, Naomi, Mary, and Martha—all of them saw God intervene to bring about his plan and purposes.

Beloved, do not be surprised at the fiery ordeal among you, which comes upon you for your testing, as though some strange thing were happening to you.

1 PETER 4:12, NASB

Casting the whole of your care [all your anxieties, all your worries, all your concerns, once and for all] on Him; for He cares for you affectionately and cares about you watchfully.

1 PETER 5:7, AMPLIFIED

Father, deliver me from this pain. While I wait for your healing, use this adversity for your glory. Work into me greater compassion for those who suffer, a desire to walk with them, and the ability to encourage them.

WHEN YOU LONG FOR DELIVERANCE

Because recovery takes time, we easily lose patience with the process. But if we are going to minister to others in their crises, it helps to have been there ourselves. In the midst of every pain, time of suffering, or personal dilemma, God will come with power to deliver. But we must invite him, then allow him to work in his own way and in his own timing.

Many women have told us that learning to offer praise to God, even when they didn't feel like it, was a major factor that helped them get through tough times.

Devotional writer Ruth Myers gives this observation:

As fire melts unrefined silver, bringing the impurities to the surface, so trials bring the "scum" to the top in your life. When you praise God in the midst of a trial, you cooperate with His plan to remove the scum; when you complain, you resist His plan and stir the impurities right back into your character.

...Through praise you focus your attention on God. You acknowledge Him as your source of overcoming power. You begin to look at your problems from a new perspective....You have a part in making them the prelude to new victories, the raw materials for God's miracles.[22]

"Woman, you are loosed from your infirmity." And He laid hands on her, and immediately she was made straight, and glorified God.

LUKE 13:12b-13, NKJV

Now after you have known God, or rather are known by God, how is it that you turn again to the weak and beggarly elements, to which you desire again to be in bondage?

GALATIANS 4:9, NKJV

Father, I want to be set free from (name your bondage), but I can't find my way out without your power. I feel trapped and powerless. Come now, Holy Spirit. I yield myself to you.

CHRIST CAME TO FREE YOU

Maybe you can identify with the woman in the Bible who had to walk bent over with her face toward the floor. For eighteen long years she had been unable to stand straight or to do much for herself. Yet she faithfully attended synagogue, no doubt lost in the crowd Sabbath after Sabbath. Jesus, noticing her plight, reached out to her with words of life and liberation. In essence he said, "Woman, you are free! Lift up your head! No more bondage!"

Can you imagine what it must have felt like to stand up straight for the first time in eighteen years? To be able to look into Jesus' eyes of love and compassion and realize, "He really cares about me!" Surely the joy of the Lord engulfed her as she began to praise and glorify God.

Are you trying to cope with chronic depression, outbursts of anger, an addiction, a painful marriage, or a broken relationship? Do you feel weighed down, as if problem after problem is stacked on your shoulders until you can hardly stand?

In other words, *are you in bondage?*

The Good News is Jesus came to set the captives free! You need not remain in the bondage that harasses you and steals your joy.

With us is the Lord our God to help us and to fight our battles.

2 CHRONICLES 32:8b

Since the children [that means us] have flesh and blood, he too shared in their humanity so that by his death he [Jesus] might destroy him who holds the power of death—that is, the devil—and free those who all their lives were held in slavery by their fear of death.

HEBREWS 2:14-15

Father, nothing is impossible with you. Nothing is too hard for you. I know that your mercy and liberating power can reach even me. Thank you that Jesus makes it possible for me truly to be set free.

JESUS, THE LIBERATOR

Jesus wants you—and the countless women we have met—set free from every bondage, just as he wanted the daughter of Abraham to be loosed. His desire to liberate us caused Jesus to come to earth in human form and make the supreme sacrifice to gain our freedom.

Because he walked this earth just like you and me, Jesus can empathize with the pain of our bondages. Because of his purity and holiness, however, his victory over sin and Satan makes our release from bondage possible.

Perhaps you feel your situation is hopeless, that your bondage is too entrenched for you ever to experience freedom. You can replace your despair with hope. Jesus can set you free.

If Jesus is your Lord, you are a cherished daughter of the King! Begin your steps out of bondage by affirming what God's Word says about you and refuse to identify with the enemy's accusations against you. Agreeing with the Word of God is one sure way to victory—over insecurity, low self-esteem, inferiority, anger, lust, or whatever captivity you find yourself in right now.

As a father has compassion on his children, so the Lord has compassion on those who fear him.... From everlasting to everlasting the Lord's love is with those who fear him.

PSALM 103:13-17

Though your sins are like scarlet, they shall be as white as snow.

ISAIAH 1:18

Father, I throw myself into your arms fully confident that you will embrace me just as I am. I can breathe easy because your Son has clothed me in righteousness. You are gracious, patient, and kind. I am safe with you.

GOD'S ARMS ARE OPEN

Many people seem to feel God's standards are unreasonably high, and they feel guilty and fearful that they can never measure up. It's true; we can never measure up in our own strength. But as the late teacher A.W. Tozer reminds us:

> The truth is that God is the most winsome of all beings ... He is all love, and those who trust Him need never know anything but that love. He is just, indeed, and He will not condone sin; but through the blood of the everlasting covenant He is able to act toward us exactly as if we had never sinned.
>
> ... Some of us are religiously jumpy and self-conscious because we know that God sees our every thought and is acquainted with all our ways. We need not be. God is the sum of all patience and the essence of kindly good will.
>
> We please Him most, not by frantically trying to make ourselves good, but by throwing ourselves into His arms with all our imperfections, and believing that He understands everything and loves us still.[23]

After receiving God's forgiveness, you must also forgive yourself if you are truly to be free from guilt. Otherwise "false guilt" turns inward and produces anger toward yourself.

83

It is for freedom that Christ has set us free. Stand firm, then, and do not let yourselves be burdened again by a yoke of slavery…. You, my brothers, were called to be free. But do not use your freedom to indulge the sinful nature; rather, serve one another in love.

GALATIANS 5:1,13

Thank you, Lord, that I am called to freedom and not to slavery, and that I will not be ensnared again with a yoke of bondage. I acknowledge that my walk with you is not all that it should be. I don't want to live a life of defeat. Please help me to identify the bondages in my life and to find the way to freedom.

OUT OF THE ENEMY'S GRIP

Bible teacher Dean Sherman defines bondage as it applies to a Christian:

If we continue in a habit of sin, we can develop a bondage. A bondage means that there is a supernatural element to our problem. The enemy now has a grip on a function of our personality. Traditionally, we have talked of a progression, with people being obsessed, oppressed, or possessed. But I have stopped using these words because it is hard to define where one stops and another begins. The word "possessed" doesn't appear in original Scriptures; the word used is simply "demonized." That is what I am calling a bondage. It is possible to have a bondage that does not consume your entire personality and function—you are merely bound in a certain part of your personality. Whatever the bondage, and whatever the degree, if you are bound, you need to be set free in Jesus' name.[24]

God does not plan for us to endure lives of quiet defeat. Yet we do have a responsibility. We don't earn our freedom by good behavior, but we must be willing to throw out the excess baggage that invites bondage. God joins his power with our will to be liberated. Then the freedom he wants us to enjoy is inevitable.

If you are angry, don't sin by nursing your grudge. Don't let the sun go down with you still angry—get over it quickly; for when you are angry you give a mighty foothold to the devil.

EPHESIANS 4:26-27, LB

My dear brothers, take note of this: Everyone should be quick to listen, slow to speak and slow to become angry, for man's anger does not bring about the righteous life that God desires.

JAMES 1:19-20

Father, I resolve to rule over my emotions with greater self-control. Show me how to deal with my anger quickly and in a healthy way. Teach me to bring it to your cross, lay it down, and walk away.

ANGER

How many people do you know who have given the devil a foothold in their lives because they have nursed a grudge or harbored anger and bitterness in their hearts? Are you in this condition yourself? Your anger, not dealt with properly, opens the door to a spirit of anger. It can become a controlling force in your life and keep you in prison.

Emotions are God-given, and expressing our emotions in healthy ways is God's plan for us. On the other hand, women often feel victimized by the strength of their emotions or the fear of them. These fears lead us to deny, repress, over-express, or manipulate our emotions instead of dealing with them head-on. Anger is perhaps hardest to handle, especially if we've stored it up only to overreact to a relatively minor infraction.

The way out of this bondage is to follow Paul's advice in Ephesians 4:26-27. Get rid of any stored-up anger, and don't allow it to accumulate in the future. With the help of the Holy Spirit, you can become like the person whom Proverbs 16:32 describes: "He who is slow to anger is better than the mighty, And he who rules his spirit, than he who captures a city"(NASB).

If anyone would come after me, he must deny him-self and take up his cross daily and follow me. For whoever wants to save his life will lose it, but who-ever loses his life for me will save it. What good is it for a man to gain the whole world, and yet lose or forfeit his very self?

LUKE 9:23-25

Father, I confess that I have wanted my own way and will-fully pursued it. I repent for my rebellion and accept responsibility for the consequences of my sin. I humbly ask that you would redeem my mistakes and make some-thing good come from these circumstances, which I have brought upon myself. I receive your forgiveness and turn from my selfish ways.

SELFISH AMBITION

Our desire to control or manipulate circumstances and people can become a pattern of behavior that may keep us from intimacy with God and ultimately lead to bondage. It is one of the biggest hindrances to freedom in the Spirit.

Many of us choose our own way over the good of others and the wisdom of God, often going against inner warnings or wise counsel. Now we face painful consequences such as financial loss or joblessness, broken relationships with family members, a difficult marriage, divorce, or the problem of rearing an out-of-wedlock child. How can we best deal with these crushing problems?

First, confess to the Lord your sin of willfulness and fully repent before him. This is a time to take full responsibility for your part in the matter, without shifting the blame to someone else.

Next, ask God to redeem your mistakes. His love and mercy can transform even the most hopeless circumstances into something positive and fruitful. The key is in being willing to submit to his ways, to receive his forgiveness for your mistakes, and to forgive yourself.

There is one who speaks rashly like the thrusts of a sword, but the tongue of the wise brings healing.

PROVERBS 12:18, NASB

Death and life are in the power of the tongue.

PROVERBS 18:21a, NASB

Father, please help me to forgive (name), who has (abused/rejected/cursed–be specific) me. (repeat for each individual to be forgiven.)

I honestly don't feel (name) deserve forgiveness, but I want my relationship with you to be right so I choose to forgive. Heal my painful memories. Help me to anticipate with joy what you have in store for my life. Your Word says you complete the good work you start (see Philippians 1:6). Thank you for not forsaking me.

THE POWER OF WORDS

Words don't leave bruises and black eyes, but they can do profound damage to the soul.

Words of rejection spoken to you and about you function like the recording head of an old-fashioned phonograph. The message is transmitted via a needle that cuts a series of grooves into the soft material of the phonograph record, which then hardens. Every time you play the record, you hear a "less than" message. You're not good enough, smart enough, pretty enough, talented enough, diligent enough ... to be accepted by your family and peers. Thus you begin to see yourself as "less than" others.

Whether we talk to ourselves or others, speaking evil or negative words that do not agree with God's Word can create bondage. Words that others speak about us or write against us—if we agree with them—keep us in bondage!

If you are struggling with the bondage of words spoken over you, begin your way to freedom by using Scripture to break the power of those words. Read aloud to yourself Scriptures that reinforce how precious, treasured, and loved you are in God's sight.

When I am afraid, I will trust in you. In God, whose word I praise, in God I trust; I will not be afraid. What can mortal man do to me?

PSALM 56:3-4

There is no fear in love. But perfect love drives out fear, because fear has to do with punishment. The one who fears is not made perfect in love.

1 JOHN 4:18

But let all those who take refuge and put their trust in You rejoice; let them ever sing and shout for joy, because You make a covering over them and defend them; let those also who love Your name be joyful in You and be in high spirits.

PSALM 5:11, AMPLIFIED

Lord, please show me if I have an unhealthy amount of fear—if I am indeed in bondage. Show me where it came in and how to rid myself of it. If I need help in resisting the evil one and walking through to victory, direct me to the right prayer partner or counselor. My desire is to walk free, no longer bound. Lord, I thank you in advance.

FEAR

All kinds of fears plague women in today's world. Some of the major ones they share with us are:

fear of being alone   *fear of the dark*

fear of financial instability   *fear of injury or violence*

fear of cancer or disabling sickness   *fear of suffering and pain*

fear of death   *fear of losing a loved one*

fear of losing a relationship   *fear of losing independence*

fear of the future

Fear. Dread. Alarm. Some women live in perpetual fear, especially for their children or husbands. Fear can be beneficial when it warns us of impending danger, but when taken to extremes and coupled with worry, it quickly becomes a heavy bondage. If we Christian women allow fear to dominate our thoughts, we're really telling God we don't trust him. We don't mean to send that message, but somehow we have gotten so caught up in fearful worry, we don't realize the depth of our bondage.

Kate, once plagued by fear, shared her steps to eventual victory: "Identify the problem, seek help, take risks by joining a support group, explore the pain, and express the fear. Keep praising God during your healing process, and through prayer release all the bondages. Then walk in victory!"

Do not get drunk on wine, which leads to debauchery. Instead, be filled with the Spirit.

EPHESIANS 5:18

So I tell you this, and insist on it in the Lord, that you must no longer live as the Gentiles do, in the futility of their thinking.... They have given themselves over to sensuality so as to indulge in every kind of impurity, with a continual lust for more.

EPHESIANS 4:17-19

Father, I realize that my cravings for (name objects) are out of control. My appetites rule over me, and I can't seem to overcome them. Apart from you I am helpless, but with your help I can do all things. Strengthen me moment by moment as I seek to overcome these lusts through the power of your Holy Spirit.

ADDICTIONS

Our human nature is basically rebellious and self-centered. Addictions are, to put it bluntly, spiritual idolatry. Addictions keep us depending on things to satisfy us rather than relying on a loving God.

Augustine once said, "Idolatry is worshiping anything that ought to be used, or using anything that ought to be worshiped."

What a warning! As Christians you and I must not place our affections on things that enslave us. The Holy Spirit can help us recognize early signs of addictive bondages.

Maybe you feel you've sunk too far, as into drug or alcohol abuse or compulsive eating, shopping, or exercising. *Oh, it's hopeless*, you think. Corrie ten Boom used to say, "There is no pit so deep but that Jesus' love is deeper still."

If you realize you do have a habit that is out of control, stop and admit your bondage, first to yourself, then to God. Now determine to get help—from a Christian counselor, a pastor, or a spiritual friend. Remember, when you call out, the Lord is always there to help and guide you. Never underestimate his power to help you recover. God extends his arms toward you. He waits for you. He is calling and asking you to turn to him.

Search me, O God, and know my heart; test me and know my anxious thoughts. See if there is any offensive way in me, and lead me in the way everlasting.

PSALM 139:23-24

Father, thank you for shining the light of the Holy Spirit into my heart and revealing to me the areas of bondage where I need deliverance. Lord Jesus, pride is not going to keep me from receiving your healing and freedom. I humble myself and confess my sins of rebellion.

(Name the areas of sin you wish to confess. Speak out what the Holy Spirit reveals. The following sentence can be repeated for each area of sin, being specific.) I renounce the sin of (name of sin) and declare it will no longer have dominion over me.

I close all doors where the enemy has gained entry, and I ask you to seal these areas with the blood of Jesus. Holy Spirit, please help me to focus my thoughts on the things of God and break my old patterns of thinking and acting.

STEPS TOWARD FREEDOM

Bondages frequently entangle God's children and render them powerless in spiritual warfare. If the devil cannot get you to renounce your faith altogether, he will try to ensnare you with traps and make you ineffective.

Such bondages are like chains holding us tightly to our past. They usually affect our mind, will, and emotions, and in turn influence our behavior.

Let us look at the steps we can take in order to walk free of such bondage:

1. Identify the problem area. Ask the Holy Spirit to show you any areas of bondage you may have overlooked.
2. Confess and repent before the Lord the sins the Holy Spirit reveals to you.
3. Choose to forgive all who have wounded you; also forgive yourself. Release your anger toward God, your feeling that he "let you down."
4. Receive God's forgiveness and cleansing.
5. Renounce the sin and close the door in any area where the enemy has gained entry.
6. Ask the Holy Spirit to help you break the behavior and thought patterns to which you've become accustomed. (See Philippians 4:7-9.)
7. Allow the Holy Spirit to daily conform you to the image of Christ.

She is a woman of strength and dignity, and has no fear of old age. When she speaks, her words are wise, and kindness is the rule for everything she says.

PROVERBS 31:25-26, LB

Father, because I am your beloved daughter, clothe me with your strength and dignity. Remove my tattered cloak of shame and weakness, and let me see myself standing radiantly robed in your righteousness. Deepen my realization and understanding of what you have done for me in Christ. Help me reflect your transforming power in the way I live my life.

STRENGTH AND DIGNITY

What is our goal? To become the persons God created us to be.

One of the scriptural models of that is the virtuous woman of Proverbs 31. The New International Version says she "is clothed with strength and dignity," the exact opposite of the cloak of shame.

Strength is the capacity to sustain force without yielding or breaking; it speaks of solidity, tenacity, and a source of power. Dignity means the state or quality of being excellent, worthy, or honorable, or having nobility of manner.

Women filled with God's spirit are women of power. Our Proverbs 31 example is not only strong, powerful, and valiant, she's dynamic in authority.

As you walk out of bondage, shedding your cloak of shame and guilt, you can model your walk with God after this virtuous woman. Think of yourself as a daughter of the King, part of a royal priesthood, and a virtuous woman with a reverential fear and love for the Lord.

For if you forgive men when they sin against you, your heavenly Father will also forgive you. But if you do not forgive men their sins, your Father will not forgive your sins.

MATTHEW 6:14-15

Then the master called the servant in. "You wicked servant," he said, "I canceled all that debt of yours because you begged me to. Shouldn't you have had mercy on your fellow servant just as I had on you?"

MATTHEW 18:32-33

Father, send your Holy Spirit to help me forgive (name). Letting go of my grievance is so difficult, but I release it to you now. Fill me with your peace and bind up my wounds with your love.

UNCHAINING OTHERS

Forgiveness through Christ is the cornerstone of our reconciliation and relationship with God. Knowing this, Satan attacks our capacity to give and receive forgiveness. He prompts us to indulge our grievances and hold on to our bitterness by telling us over and over, "The person who did this to you doesn't deserve to be forgiven!" Unwillingness to forgive will sentence you to bondage and torment, and the person you refuse to forgive remains bound also.

Dr. Norman Wright, in discussing the importance of a daughter forgiving her father, gives this graphic picture:

> Forgiveness involves letting go. Remember playing tug-of-war as a child? As long as the parties on each end of the rope are tugging, you have a "war." But when someone lets go, the war is over. When you forgive your father, you are letting go of your end of the rope. No matter how hard he may tug on the other end, if you have released your end, the war is over for you.[25]

No freedom can compare to that which comes when we decide to set at liberty anyone against whom we've held a grudge. One person's decision to forgive has power to open prison doors for those in hopeless bondage.

Do not judge, and you will not be judged. Do not condemn, and you will not be condemned. Forgive, and you will be forgiven.

LUKE 6:37

Bear with each other and forgive whatever grievances you may have against one another. Forgive as the Lord forgave you.

COLOSSIANS 3:13

Father, your Son paid the huge debt I owed to you. Jesus took my punishment and restored my innocence, forgiving me of all my sin. Now please help me to forgive myself. May your gift of forgiveness always remind me to be quick to forgive others. Thank you, Lord!

WE FORGIVE, GOD HEALS

If you are suffering due to rejection, abandonment, or betrayal, remember the Lord Jesus knew what it was like to be betrayed by those close to him. He can identify with your hurts and wounds.

Forgiveness is not a onetime choice; it is ongoing and progressive. You deal with one layer at a time. Some of us need to forgive ourselves, even for sins that date way back. If that's your situation, accept Jesus' love and forgiveness right now. Then forgive yourself, and don't let yesterday rob you of today.

"After I'd forgiven Robert, I had flashbacks which focused on me: my sinfulness, rebellion, and disobedience," Esther told us. "With every memory I would confess, repent of my sin, and receive God's forgiveness. Over the next six months, I was able to put regret behind me. Within a year I was free from the bondage of the relationship."

Identifying the areas of hurt and disappointment and placing them in God's hands allows him to begin changing you. Don't be surprised if he fills you with tears that wash over you with floods of his peace and healing. As you yield to the Holy Spirit, his love will begin to radiate through you.

Contend, O Lord, with those who contend with me;
fight against those who fight against me. Take up
shield and buckler; arise and come to my aid.

PSALM 35:1-2

You have heard that it was said, "Love your neigh-
bor and hate your enemy." But I tell you: Love your
enemies and pray for those who persecute you, that
you may be sons of your Father in heaven.

MATTHEW 5:43-45

Father, I choose to love my enemies with your love and to pray for them. I will look upon (name these people) as victims of the enemy in desperate need of your love and transforming grace. I will become an intercessor on their behalf just as Christ is for me.

LOVE THOSE ENEMIES

Who among us has not been harassed by a boss, neighbor, or relative? Who hasn't felt betrayed by a friend? Or unfairly treated or falsely accused by a teacher, supervisor, or even a church leader? Some of us have even been the target of an unfounded lawsuit.

Not only does God come to our rescue when we are harassed, but because we belong to him, his favor shines upon us. You may feel you have been misunderstood and never had your name or reputation cleared, but God is the one who keeps the records, not our fellow human beings.

We need to remember to turn to our heavenly Father for strength and wisdom in the midst of attack. He will truly enable us to love our enemies and pray for them. Who knows? Perhaps the verbal attack is the very crack in the door through which Jesus can enter your accuser's heart. Seize the opportunity to do spiritual battle for the Lord.

Forgive us our debts, as we also have forgiven our debtors. And lead us not into temptation, but deliver us from the evil one.

MATTHEW 6:12-13

Father, the offenses of others against me shrink to nothing in the light of your loving forgiveness of all my sin. Help me to keep this perspective in every painful relationship that I have with others.

DON'T PASS TRASH

Children in their naiveté sometimes express profound truth in the simplest of words—or even made-up words. Ruthanne's husband came home from a weekend preaching trip recently and shared a new version of the Lord's Prayer from a pastor's young son: "Forgive us our trash-passes, as we forgive those who pass trash against us...."

To forgive means to give up the desire to get even or to "pass trash" against someone. It means to renounce anger and resentment, to release one's debtor. It is a decision made with the will. We can *decide* to forgive the person who has offended us, whether we feel like it or not.

We put forgiveness in its proper perspective when we realize that any injustice we have suffered from another person is small compared to our own sin against God. In other words, the "trash" we've passed against our loving, heavenly Father is much worse than all the "trash" others have passed against us!

When we fail to forgive, we bind ourselves to the continuing pain that results from holding onto the grievance. It shows in our faces, in the slump of our shoulders, even in our conversation.

Get rid of all bitterness, rage and anger, brawling and slander, along with every form of malice. Be kind and compassionate to one another, forgiving each other, just as in Christ God forgave you.

Be imitators of God, therefore, as dearly loved children and live a life of love, just as Christ loved us and gave himself up for us a fragrant offering and sacrifice to God.

EPHESIANS 4:31-32; 5:1-2

Lord, I truly mean it when I pray, "Forgive us our debts, as we also have forgiven our debtors" (Matthew 6:12). Thank you for helping me work my way through the process of forgiving those who have wounded me.

ONGOING FORGIVENESS

Paul was writing to Christians in Ephesians, and it is clear by his language that they needed to deal with the grievances and hard feelings they had toward one another. He reminds them that forgiving each other is the solution to their conflicts as well as their protection against the devil's strategy. And it's our protection, too.

Continual, unresolved conflict with a difficult person can seriously traumatize your life. It may cause or contribute to chronic physical problems, such as asthma, ulcers, arthritis, migraines, and muscle spasms. Or it may show up in emotional problems, such as panic attacks, learning disabilities, eating disorders, and so on.

A personal acquaintance is an example of the destructive toll unforgiveness exacts from people's lives. She suffered emotionally and physically, lost her marriage, and was alienated from her daughters and mother-in-law. She attributes these losses to the root of bitterness she harbored against her mother-in-law. She finally forgave, however, and her mother-in-law is in heaven today and she herself is healed and now able to touch other women's lives with healing.

God deals with each of his children on an individual basis in this process of forgiving. He always does it in love. But it is the major key to walking free from bondage.

The Lord is compassionate and gracious, slow to anger, abounding in love.... He does not treat us as our sins deserve or repay us according to our iniquities.

PSALM 103:8, 10

Judgment without mercy will be shown to anyone who has not been merciful. Mercy triumphs over judgment!

JAMES 2:13

Father, I choose to forgive (name) for (name the offenses), and I release (him/her) from my judgment. Lord, help me to see (name) from your point of view. I ask you to judge (him/her) according to your mercy and to grant (name) healing and release from bondage.

Thank you, Lord, for the mercy you have shown by forgiving my sins. Help me choose to forgive each time a painful memory comes back or someone offends me. I rejoice in the freedom forgiveness brings to my life!

TAKING THE RIGHT STEPS

Perhaps the most important thing to understand about forgiving is this: it is a process, more than an isolated occurrence.

"We might make a blanket statement like, 'I forgive my father,' but we need to forgive specifically," a counselor friend says. Her suggestion is that in prayer you say something such as: "God, I forgive Dad for not being there when I needed him, for touching me improperly, for beating me, for not showing love, for being mean to my mom, for dying and abandoning me," or whatever the situation.

In some cases it's helpful to make a list of everything you didn't get or didn't get enough of from your mother, father, husband, or any person who wounded you. You may need to list all the reasons you are still angry with that person. Then, for each circumstance, go to God in prayer and forgive specifically the things you have listed.

If possible, it is beneficial to talk these things over with a counselor or a prayer partner and to have them pray with you. Sharing with a person you can trust helps you to let out your feelings. It also makes you accountable to someone who can help you see the situation objectively.

Miriam the prophetess, Aaron's sister, took a tambourine in her hand, and all the women followed her, with tambourines and dancing. Miriam sang to them: "Sing to the Lord, for he is highly exalted. The horse and its rider he has hurled into the sea."

EXODUS 15:20-21

Now bands from Aram had gone out and had taken captive a young girl from Israel, and she served Naaman's wife. She said to her mistress, "If only my master would see the prophet who is in Samaria! He would cure him of his leprosy."

2 KINGS 5:2-3

Father, thank you for making me your daughter and for showing me in your Word how you have used your women for your glory. May I follow in this line of women who served, loved, and believed in you.

ORDINARY WOMEN, EXTRAORDINARY PURPOSES

I (Quin) love to read Bible stories about how God uses women to accomplish something for him regardless of how insignificant they may seem to others.

- Miriam leads the women in a celebration song and dance when Pharaoh's chariots with their horsemen are thrown into the sea.
- A Hebrew slave in the household of the commander of Syria's army sends him to the prophet Elisha for healing of his leprosy. One woman interceding.
- With the promise to dedicate him to the Lord, Hannah begs God for a son, then releases her boy Samuel to train in the temple and become a prophet.

Ordinary women like you and me. The New Testament tells about a lot of them. Martha serves Jesus meals while Mary sits at his feet. Women minister to Jesus with their money and talents. The Samaritan woman at the well has just one encounter with Jesus, then runs to tell all her village about the Messiah.

Whenever I wonder whether my prayers or ministry make any difference, I reread these stories of women whom God used and whose prayers he heard, and I realize once again that God has gifted each of us with a unique call and talent.

Come, see a man who told me everything I ever did.
Could this be the Christ?

JOHN 4:29

The angel said to the women,... "He is not here; he
has risen, just as he said." ... So the women hurried
away from the tomb, afraid yet filled with joy, and
ran to tell his disciples. Suddenly Jesus met them....
Then Jesus said to them, "Do not be afraid. Go and
tell my brothers to go to Galilee; there they will see
me."

MATTHEW 28:5a, 6a, 8, 9a, 10

Father, thank you for creating me as a woman and for showing me my great value to you. May I never shrink back from your purposes for my life. You have crowned me with love and compassion as your daughter.

JESUS' INNER CIRCLE

When Jesus had an encounter with the Samaritan woman at the well, she hurried to her village to tell everyone. Many people believed in him because of her testimony. Then Jesus himself went there and taught for two days, and many more became believers. (See John 4:1-41.)

We read that many women followed Jesus during his earthly ministry and ministered to him. Can you imagine what it might have been like to have been in that group of "certain women" who were in Jesus' inner circle?

- A woman, Anna, had at his birth proclaimed him to be the Messiah. (See Luke 2:36-38.)
- The inner circle of women followed him to the cross, with many others, but they were the last to remain there. (See Luke 23:49.)
- Two devoted women were the first to come to the tomb to minister to him. (See Mark 16:1.)
- Thus it was women who had the privilege of first proclaiming the news of the resurrection. (See Matthew 28:8.)

Jesus clearly valued women, and he elevated their status for all time by the way he, a Jewish teacher, honored them. Women also waited in the Upper Room for the promise of the Father, were filled with the Holy Spirit, spoke in tongues, and participated in the commission to "go and tell."

On that day Deborah ... sang this song: "... May all your enemies perish, O Lord! But may they who love you be like the sun when it rises in its strength."

JUDGES 5:1, 31

The Lord gives the command; The women who proclaim the good tidings are a great host: "Kings of armies flee, they flee, And she who remains at home will divide the spoil!"

PSALM 68:11-12, NASB

Esther again pleaded with the king, falling at his feet and weeping. She begged him to put an end to the evil plan against the Jews. Then the king extended the gold scepter to Esther and she arose and stood before him.

ESTHER 8:3-4

Father, I pray that you will find me a bold and obedient soldier. May I fight the good fight, as Deborah and Esther did, through the power of your Spirit and for your glory.

GOD WANTS A GREAT ARMY OF WOMEN

Where are the Deborahs and Esthers of our generation?

The Deborahs are those who will get God's instructions and go to war against the enemy, confident that God goes before them. The Esthers are those who will intercede before the king on behalf of their people, those who will pay the price to get a wicked proclamation reversed.

Nancy Clarke writes in Women's Aglow *Connection:*

> We Christians are the people of God, empowered by him to defeat Satan's forces and the stronghold they have in the minds and hearts of men. God depends on us to deliver the power blow so that, as we reach out to hurting people in our communities, they will be open to hear his message. God has an army forming to help open the way in the midst of the war zones in which we live. Time is wasting. Join up now.[26]

How true this is of spiritual warfare! Our liberation began with Jesus' death, burial, and resurrection. Our Savior, the seed of the woman, crushed Satan's head and broke his power. Now it's up to us to exert the authority Jesus invested in us to take back the ground the enemy has stolen. We have nothing to fear!

*The Lord is my light and my salvation—whom shall
I fear? The Lord is the stronghold of my life—of
whom shall I be afraid?*

PSALM 27:1

*Through God we will do valiantly,
For it is He who shall tread down our enemies.*

PSALM 108:13, NKJV

Lord, may I be as that brave woman whose aim with her
millstone knocked out the enemy. Give me strategic ways
to pray to disarm the enemy's plan. Help me to pray specifically and on target to accomplish what is on your heart. I
ask this in Jesus' name.

FEATS OF SUPERHUMAN STRENGTH

We've all heard stories of a woman performing feats of superhuman strength, such as lifting the back of a car when her child was in danger. The maternal instinct sends a surge of adrenaline through a woman, empowering her to do something thought impossible even for a well-muscled man. How much greater is the power the Holy Spirit gives to enable us in spiritual warfare.

I (Quin) like the account in the Old Testament about the Israelite woman who, when she saw King Abimelech approaching her city to burn it, took immediate and decisive action. Watching him from the top of the Tower of Thebez, she picked up an upper millstone and hurled it down on the wicked king's head. Too proud to have it said that a woman killed him, the king ordered his armor bearer to draw his sword and finish him off. (See Judges 9:50-57; 2 Samuel 11:21.)

Never let it be said that women are weak! They are still hurling stones at the enemy's plans. This unnamed woman of Thebez is one of a large company of women who continue to wreak havoc on Satan's plans.

Likewise, teach the older women to be reverent in the way they live, not to be slanderers or addicted to much wine, but to teach what is good. Then they can train the younger women to love their husbands and children, to be self-controlled and pure, to be busy at home, to be kind, and to be subject to their husbands, so that no one will malign the word of God.

TITUS 2:3-5

Father, I know you desire to help me mature through the sisters in the Lord whom I allow to speak into my life. Lead me to a woman who has a heart for you and wisdom to offer me as I seek to live my life fully for you.

Lord, make me sensitive to the needs of younger women in my church, neighborhood, and community. Show me practical ways of encouraging and supporting them and loving them with your love.

WOMEN TRAINING WOMEN

Have you ever imagined the mentoring that went on woman-to-woman in the Bible accounts?

- Naomi repeatedly referred to her daughter-in-law Ruth as "my daughter," and we know she taught her about spiritual things. (See Ruth 1:11, 12, 13.)
- Think of the older woman Elizabeth, while pregnant with John the Baptist, mentoring her young relative, the virgin Mary, who awaited the birth of the Messiah she carried in her womb. (See Luke 1:35-56.)
- Lois was a woman who instilled spiritual truths into her daughter Eunice, who had a son named Timothy. Together, grandmother and mother had an impact on this young evangelist whom Paul highly treasured. (See 2 Timothy 1:5.)
- Dorcas, a well-known seamstress, was resurrected after her untimely death through the prayers of Peter because her ministry was so needed. (See Acts 9.) Have you ever thought of all the others she might have mentored—or taught to sew?

The Holy Spirit can teach you through Scripture and encourage you in the stresses of daily life to exhibit the fruit of the Spirit. But when he provides a mentor to speak into your life on a regular basis, the process is easier, and it makes you accountable to someone more mature in the Lord.

Most important of all, continue to show deep love for each other, for love makes up for many of your faults. Cheerfully share your home with those who need a meal or a place to stay for the night.

God has given each of you some special abilities; be sure to use them to help each other, passing on to others God's many kinds of blessings.

1 PETER 4:8-10, LB

Father, I open the doors of my home to you and to those for whom you want me to care. Give me a generous spirit and spontaneity that comes from gratitude for all that you have given me. Teach me through the example of other women how to be gracious and how to serve without complaint.

HOSPITALITY: A SANCTUARY IN THE BATTLE

While you may never travel far, God will put people in your path whom you can influence for him.

One of the best ways modern-day Christian women can proclaim the Good News is through hospitality. Using our homes to touch our friends and neighbors, we may reach people who would never enter a church.

After the outpouring of the Holy Spirit on the day of Pentecost, believers began meeting in homes to devote themselves to these four things (see Acts 2:42-47):

- the apostles' teaching
- fellowship
- breaking of bread
- prayer

The homes of those in the Early Church became sanctuaries for teaching, prayer, fellowship, and meals. Hospitality—reaching out to those whom God puts in your path—is an effective way to win others to the Lord.

Though Peter was encouraging Christians to help other believers, if we are full of God's love, we will find creative ways to use our homes as avenues of sharing the gospel. As in the early church, our homes also can be "little sanctuaries." How many times have you had others come into your home and say, "I feel peace here." Or, "I just like to come into your house—it's so restful." Why is that? Hopefully because the presence of the Lord is there.

The Lord God said, "It is not good for the man to be alone. I will make a helper suitable for him." ...Then the Lord God made a woman from the rib he had taken out of the man, and he brought her to the man.

GENESIS 2:18, 22

[Jesus replied,] "For this reason a man will leave his father and mother and be united to his wife, and the two will become one flesh. So they are no longer two, but one. Therefore what God has joined together, let man not separate."

MARK 10:7-9

Father, you know the areas of my marriage that are most vulnerable to the attack of the evil one. Reveal these areas to my husband and me and show us through your Holy Spirit how to fight for and protect our marriage. May our marriage be full of your love and unfailing commitment. May we stand firm together in you.

GUARD YOUR MARRIAGE

Marriage, family, and home were God's plan from the beginning of creation. Since God initiated marriages, Satan does anything possible to interfere with godly marriages and to damage relationships between righteous people.

Paul teaches that God intended marriage to be a picture of the relationship between Christ and his church. (See Ephesians 5:21-23.) Is it any wonder that Satan lashes out at marriages, trying to destroy them? Or that he tries to ravage the fruit of marriage, our children? God wants us to be aware of Satan's schemes and guard against them. (See 2 Corinthians 2:11, Ephesians 6:11.)

Dr. Archibald Hart writes:

> Since our relationship with our spouse is to be our sole sexual focus, this is where we need to direct our attention. Building a good marriage is hard work. Every marriage begins with the union of two incompatible people in an impossible relationship. The task God gives us in marriage is to turn it into something beautiful. With God's grace—it *can* be done.[27]

Christian couples must make it a priority to pray together, to walk in mutual forgiveness, and to keep their communication with one another open and honest.

Submit to one another out of reverence for Christ.

EPHESIANS 5:21

Each of you also must love his wife as he loves himself, and the wife must respect her husband.

EPHESIANS 5:33

Father, I bring to you the (list your struggles) in my marriage. Give me and my husband wisdom to deal with these problem areas. Give us resources to resolve our conflicts. Give us willing and forgiving spirits so our marriage can grow stronger in you.

ENEMY FOOTHOLDS IN MARRIAGE

Perhaps you and your spouse are both Christians, usually compatible, and you share fairly common goals. Yet you can see yourself in one or more of the following situations. In fact, you may be deeply concerned about how often you:

- Find yourself bickering with your mate over relatively minor matters, then holding a grudge afterwards.
- Find yourself saying or hearing "why are you always late?" (or some other negative "always" or "never" expression).
- Feel resentment when your spouse is more polite or attentive to others (especially of the opposite sex) than to you.
- Find that your spouse is sure to misunderstand if you try to express your true feelings—so you stifle them.
- Realize you've been comparing your companion unfavorably with a former sweetheart or a current acquaintance.
- Find yourself wanting to conceal from your partner certain friendships, purchases, or ways you spend your time.

These are problems with which many Christian partners struggle. If not confronted and dealt with through prayer, asking and granting forgiveness, or seeking godly counsel, such problems may start out seemingly small but end up consuming a relationship. They are footholds the devil will exploit in an effort to destroy marriages.

Open their eyes and turn them from darkness to light, and from the power of Satan to God, so that they may receive forgiveness of sins and a place among those who are sanctified by faith in me [Jesus].

ACTS 26:18

But do not forget this one thing, dear friends: With the Lord a day is like a thousand years, and a thousand years are like a day. The Lord is not slow in keeping his promise, as some understand slowness. He is patient with you, not wanting anyone to perish, but everyone to come to repentance.

2 PETER 3:8-9

Praise be to the God and Father of our Lord Jesus Christ, who has blessed us in the heavenly realms with every spiritual blessing in Christ. For he chose us in him before the creation of the world to be holy and blameless in his sight. In love he predestined us to be adopted as his sons through Jesus Christ, in accordance with his pleasure and will—to the praise of his glorious grace, which he has freely given us in the One he loves. In him we have redemption through his blood, the forgiveness of sins, in accordance with the riches of God's grace that he lavished on us with all wisdom and understanding.

EPHESIANS 1:1-8

HOW TO PRAY FOR YOUR UNBELIEVING HUSBAND

Lord, my husband doesn't know you, and it grieves me so. I know you love him and that Jesus came and died to save the lost. Open my husband's eyes so that he may see the truth, which is Jesus. I pray he will see Jesus in my life. Help me to see him with your eyes and love him with your love.

In the name of Jesus I bind all evil spirits that are keeping him from knowing his heavenly Father. Lord, I pray you will send a godly man to share the gospel with him in a way he can understand and receive.

Father, grant him repentance leading to the knowledge of the truth, that he may come to his senses and escape from the snare of the devil, having been held captive by him to do his will. Lord, open his eyes so that he can turn from darkness to light and from the dominion of Satan to your kingdom, in order that he may receive forgiveness of sins and an inheritance among those who have been sanctified by faith in you. (Based on 2 Timothy 2:25b-26; Acts 26:18, NASB). Thank you, Lord, for working in his life until this prayer is answered.

All your sons will be taught by the Lord, and great will be your children's peace.

ISAIAH 54:13

Train a child in the way he should go, and when he is old he will not turn from it.

PROVERBS 22:6

But from everlasting to everlasting the Lord's love is with those who fear him, and his righteousness with their children's children.

PSALM 103:17

Father, remind me to pray your Word for my children instead of becoming anxious for them. Give me greater vision of the power of a parent's prayer to turn the hearts of children to you. Teach me to be fervent in prayer and full of trust in your excellent plan for each of my children. I know you love them, Lord, and I commit them to your care.

STANDING FOR YOUR CHILDREN

What does God desire for our children? Scripture provides many answers concerning the heart of our heavenly Father toward his little ones.

1. That Jesus Christ be formed in our children. (See Galatians 4:19.)

2. That our children—the seed of the righteous—will be delivered from the Evil One. (See Proverbs 11:21, KJV; Matthew 6:13.)

3. That our children will be taught of the Lord and their peace will be great. (See Isaiah 54:13.)

4. That they will train themselves to discern good from evil and have a good conscience before God. (See Hebrews 5:14; 1 Peter 3:21.)

5. That God's laws will be in their minds and on their hearts. (See Hebrews 8:10.)

6. That they will choose companions who are wise—not fools, nor sexually immoral, nor drunkards, nor idolaters, nor slanderers, nor swindlers. (See Proverbs 13:20; 1 Corinthians 5:11.)

7. That they will remain sexually pure and keep themselves only for their spouse, asking God for his grace to keep such a commitment. (See Ephesians 5:3, 31-33.)

8. That they will honor their parents. (See Ephesians 6:1-3.)

Many other Scriptures could be added to this list, a list that will change over time as God shows you new ways to pray his Word. Ask God for specific promises on which to stand during difficult situations.

PART THREE:

MARKS of SPIRITUAL POWER

The fruit of the Spirit is love, joy, peace, patience, kindness, goodness, faithfulness, gentleness, and self-control.... Since we live by the Spirit, let us keep in step with the Spirit.

GALATIANS 5:22-23, 25

Let us not become weary in doing good, for at the proper time we will reap a harvest if we do not give up.

GALATIANS 6:9

Father, take me deeper into your love each day, and show me the areas where my life is producing weeds and thorns. Help me to yield to the Holy Spirit's work in my heart so I can have a deeply satisfying relationship with you.

CULTIVATING GOOD FRUIT

Many Christians can probably recite from memory the list of the fruits of the Spirit mentioned in Scripture: *love, joy, peace, patience, kindness, goodness, faithfulness, gentleness, and self-control.* When present in a Christian's life, these qualities reflect a deeply satisfying relationship with the Lord, a confidence in his care and provision that generates a serene way of life. Yet many of us feel this kind of living eludes us as we measure our own flaws against what we perceive as beautiful fruit in someone else's life.

How can we cooperate with the Holy Spirit's work to cultivate fruit in our lives and rid us of all the junk that harms us? First, acknowledge that only the Holy Spirit working through us can produce fruit. Left to our own devices, we produce weeds, thorns, and thistles.

Second, recognize that cultivating fruit is not an event but a process. Being born into the kingdom is an event; it happens instantly when we believe in Christ and receive his forgiveness from sin. However, becoming a mature, fruit-bearing Christian takes place over time as we resist doing things our own way and yield to the ways of the Holy Spirit.

God has poured out his love into our hearts by the Holy Spirit, whom he has given us.

ROMANS 5:5b

Be completely humble and gentle; be patient, bearing with one another in love.

EPHESIANS 4:2

Holy Spirit, as I open my heart to my Father's unconditional love, help me to share that same quality of love with my family, neighbors, colleagues, and brothers and sisters in the Lord. Increase my capacity to be patient, kind, and forgiving, especially toward those who challenge my natural ability to love.

LOVE

How can we love the unlovable? We can't, but the Holy Spirit in us can. I (Quin) remember times when a friend or family member hurt or disappointed me and I'd cry, "Lord, make Romans 5:5 real in my life. I need help now!" At that moment I didn't sense any "natural" love toward the person because of my hurt feelings. It is at just such times, though, that we can call upon the Holy Spirit to help us love others with the love of God, which he pours into us.

"I became so dissatisfied with my husband's worldly lifestyle that I began to pray, 'God, change him!'" Carolyn told us. "But one day the Holy Spirit seemed to say, *'Carolyn, ask God to change you.'*

"Although it was difficult at first, I began asking the Lord to do a heart-change in me. I knew I needed the fruit of love in my life. Soon I was aware that my attitude really was changing. I was beginning to respond to Mark with more love. And the kinder I became toward him, the less sharp he was toward me."

Love seeks the highest good of others, regardless of their behavior—the same unconditional love God expressed for the world by sending his Son.

Let us throw off everything that hinders and the sin that so easily entangles, and let us run with perseverance the race marked out for us. Let us fix our eyes on Jesus, the author and perfecter of our faith, who for the joy set before him endured the cross, scorning its shame, and sat down at the right hand of the throne of God.

HEBREWS 12:1-2

Father, being joyful during times of difficulty and sorrow seems almost impossible to me. Show me the way through frustration and despair to your joy that will hold me steady no matter what happens. Give me the long view that Jesus had, so that the joy of my ultimate destination will overshadow any temporary troubles.

J O Y

One of the attributes of the Holy Spirit is to bring joy. Even in the midst of difficulties, "... the joy of the Lord is your strength" (Nehemiah 8:10b). How can we find joy like that? Again, Jesus is our example. He was able to endure great suffering because he knew that to fulfill his purpose on earth would bring great joy. The strength of that vision is what sustained him.

Love and joy are "marks of spiritual power," says author Richard J. Foster. He also reminds us, "The rich inner joy of spiritual power knows sorrow and is acquainted with grief. Joy and anguish often have a symbiotic relationship."[28]

We can ask the Holy Spirit to help us keep focused on our purpose in life, and with that vision in mind, sustain our joy even in the midst of adversity. Such joy can cause a genuine "makeover," both of our inner being and of our outward demeanor.

"Peace I leave with you; my peace I give you. I do not give to you as the world gives. Do not let your hearts be troubled and do not be afraid."

JOHN 14:27

"I have told you these things, so that in me you may have peace. In this world you will have trouble. But take heart! I have overcome the world."

JOHN 16:33

Let the peace of Christ rule in your hearts.

COLOSSIANS 3:15

Jesus, I long to receive the peace you offer me. Often I am troubled by circumstances and afraid of the future. I cast all this anxiety on you, knowing that you deeply care for me. You are in complete control. Now may your peace fill my heart and mind.

PEACE

Peace describes harmonious relationships between persons and between nations, freedom from molestation, friendliness, or harmonious relationships between God and man. For the Christian, peace is an inner calmness, a stillness, a quiet abiding and dependence upon the Holy Spirit. The words Jesus spoke to his followers before his death still speak to us today: "Peace I leave with you; my peace I give you...."

Marge and Ken experienced one of the most tragic losses any parent could imagine: they lost their three children in one heart-shattering blow. Yet today, twenty-five years later, they will tell you they have known first-hand God's faithfulness.

"At the funeral home [the evening after the accident] more than fifteen hundred people came to pay their respects," Marge shared. "I was so saturated with God's strength, I ended up comforting some who had come to comfort me. My constant awareness of his presence was like a warm peace radiating from my body to all I touched."

When all around you seems in turmoil, the Lord can give you his peace in the midst of the storm. In fact, peace is much more meaningful when it exists in contrast with the surrounding chaos.

Be joyful in hope, patient in affliction, faithful in prayer.

ROMANS 12:12

See how the farmer waits for the land to yield its valuable crop and how patient he is for the autumn and spring rains. You too, be patient and stand firm, because the Lord's coming is near.

JAMES 5:7b-8

Thank you, Father, for being patient with me as I have struggled with sin and fallen short of your desires for me. You have never forsaken me, never lost your vision for me, never stopped loving me. Lord, may my gratitude to you be expressed in my patience and long-suffering toward others.

PATIENCE

The Greek word that is sometimes rendered *patience* and sometimes as *long-suffering* is always used in relation to one's forbearance toward others. We need Spirit-empowering to forbear, or "put up with," those who require an extra measure of our patience and loving-kindness. (See Colossians 1:11.) This Spirit-empowered forbearance is the antidote to outbursts of rage or provoking one another.[29] (See Galatians 5:20, 26.)

Eileen Wallis shares her own difficult experience of developing this Christlike quality:

> I had to learn this during the extremely trying years I cared for my elderly mother-in-law, whose mind had failed. I felt imprisoned by circumstances beyond my control and was desperate to escape the constant restrictions. My patience dried up completely.
>
> … I was looking for freedom through escape, but God wanted me to find freedom in the situation. This liberation began the moment I recognized that my all-wise, all-loving heavenly Father was in control. He was using these circumstances as part of a beauty therapy I hadn't realized I needed. I was able to say, "Okay, Lord, I'll hand over my rights and delight to do Your will."
>
> The situation didn't change. But I did. In that act of submission I had accepted the yoke of Christ, and I could face the trial with a new peace.[30]

Therefore, as God's chosen people, holy and dearly loved, clothe yourselves with compassion, kindness, humility, gentleness, and patience. Bear with each other.

COLOSSIANS 3:12-13a

Father, teach me to be kind when I am tempted to be mean. Teach me to be gentle when I am tempted to be harsh. Teach me to want your very best for others, even when their best costs me. Help me to see goodness instead of being critical.

KINDNESS

Kindness is sweetness of disposition, gentleness in dealing with others, or benevolence. The word "kindness" describes our ability to be concerned for the welfare of those taxing our patience. The Holy Spirit removes abrasive qualities from our character if we are submitted to his control.[31]

Sometimes the fruit of kindness seems more difficult to show toward family members than toward anyone else. A woman named Margaret told us that before she received the Holy Spirit, she was very critical of her husband, Eric. Then a friend spent time in their home and praised Eric for every little thing he did.

"The Holy Spirit began to convict me for my negative expectations," Margaret said, "and gave me the idea of writing down all the good things my husband was doing. As I focused on these things, my negative expectations became less and less. Now I can easily express kindness to Eric, and praise and bless him. The change has produced a much greater measure of peace and love in our home."

Make every effort to add to your faith goodness; and to goodness, knowledge; and to knowledge, self-control; and to self-control, perseverance; and to perseverance, godliness; and to godliness, brotherly kindness; and to brotherly kindness, love. For if you possess these qualities … they will keep you from being ineffective and unproductive.

2 PETER 1:5-8

Father, I want my character to reflect your goodness and to express itself in service toward those you bring into my life. May these people feel comfortable with me because I am honorable, merciful, and caring. If I say I will do something but am tempted to cave in on my promise, convict me. I want to be faithful to you all of my days.

GOODNESS AND
FAITHFULNESS

Goodness refers to excellence of character and morals, the quality of being good, or exemplifying good behavior—closely allied with kindness. This fruit helps us overcome selfish ambition.

Dr. Gordon Fee says,

If long-suffering means not to 'chew someone's head off' (see Galations 5:15), kindness means to find ways actively to show mercy to them, to take a towel and wash basin in hand and wash their feet.... Indeed, goodness does not exist apart from its active, concrete expression.[32]

A faithful person is trustworthy in performing his duties; he fulfills his promises; he is loyal. Faithfulness is the quality which enables the believer to live out his trust in God over the long haul.[33]

God's flawless record of being faithful to us should inspire us always to be faithful to him. The psalmist proclaimed, "But you, O Lord, are a compassionate and gracious God, slow to anger, abounding in love and faithfulness" (Psalm 86:15). And Jesus, our example, was faithful even unto death.

A gentle answer turns away wrath,
but a harsh word stirs up anger.
… Like a city whose walls are broken down
is a man who lacks self-control.

PROVERBS 15:1; 25:28

For the grace of God that brings salvation has
appeared to all men. It teaches us to say "No" to
ungodliness and worldly passions, and to live self-
controlled, upright and godly lives in this present age,
while we wait for the blessed hope—the glorious
appearing of our great God and Savior, Jesus Christ,
who gave himself for us.

TITUS 2:11-14

Father, because I want to be controlled by your Spirit, I submit humbly to your training. Teach me your gentle ways. In (list areas of your life) I fail to exhibit self-control. Lord, my fleshly desires sometimes overwhelm me, and I succumb to defeat. Give me a repentant heart and a desire to change.

GENTLENESS AND SELF-CONTROL

To be gentle means to be submissive to the will of God, to be humble and teachable—not too proud to learn, and to be considerate toward others. William Barclay says, "What throws most light on its meaning is that the adjective [form of the word] is used of an animal that has been tamed and brought under control; and so the word speaks of that self-control which Christ alone can give."[34]

While the other virtues listed as fruits of the Spirit have to do with community and social relationships, this last one has to do with the inner life of individual believers. The root word means "dominion, power, or strength" and basically means to have one's faculties or energies under control of the will.[35]

This fruit is the antidote for the sexual sins as well as the sins of excess, such as drunkenness, orgies, and so forth. Total abstinence or asceticism is not the answer here, for that approach too easily turns into legalism.

Critics sometimes have faulted charismatic believers for teaching that deliverance from demonic spirits easily solves the problems of overeating, drinking, and other addictions. In some cases deliverance may be needed, but to develop the fruit of self-control, you must choose to appropriate the Holy Spirit's power to gain control over sinful inclinations.

Remain in me, and I will remain in you. No branch can bear fruit by itself; it must remain in the vine. Neither can you bear fruit unless you remain in me. I am the vine; you are the branches. If a man remains in me and I in him, he will bear much fruit; apart from me you can do nothing.

JOHN 15:4-5

My grace is sufficient for you, for my power is made perfect in weakness.

2 CORINTHIANS 12:9

Lord, I acknowledge that apart from you I am doomed to failure. Help me to abide in you and receive your empowerment to exhibit your character traits. I want the fruit in my life to be pleasing to you in every way.

FRUIT-BEARING

Bible commentator Herbert Lockyer reminds us how the Holy Spirit does his work in us:

> The Holy Spirit always produces a nobler standard of work than the flesh. And such an outcome does not come through human power but from a holy Presence pervading the life. The fruit of the Spirit is character rather than conduct—being rather than doing.
>
> … Another aspect of fruit is that it does not exist for its own sake or even for the sake of the tree, but for the support, strength, and refreshment of those who care to gather the fruit. Christ, as the Vine, did not live unto Himself. Himself He did not save. If we live for our own sake, we live in vain.[36]

The qualities mentioned as the fruit of the Spirit are character traits which Jesus' life perfectly exemplified. Such fruit does not grow in a sheltered greenhouse. It develops and thrives in everyday situations as we allow the Holy Spirit to help us pattern our attitudes and behavior toward others after Jesus' example.

Becoming a mature, fruit-bearing Christian takes place over time as we resist doing things our own way and yeild to the ways of the Holy Spirit.

When the day of Pentecost came, they were all together in one place. Suddenly a sound like the blowing of a violent wind came from heaven and filled the whole house where they were sitting. They saw what seemed to be tongues of fire that separated and came to rest on each of them. All of them were filled with the Holy Spirit.

ACTS 2:1-4

I will pour out my Spirit on all people.

ACTS 2:17

Father, I long to experience your nearness to me and my dearness to you. Send your Holy Comforter to me now. Fill my soul with assurance and joy. I open my heart to you.

DRAWING NEAR

Historical evidence reveals that the fire of the Holy Spirit was never extinguished throughout the history of the church, though it ebbed very low at times.[37]

During the revivals of the Great Awakening in the eighteenth century, various manifestations were reported by people who were touched by the Holy Spirit. Jonathan Edwards' wife, Sarah, wrote of a seventeen-day period during the outpouring of the Spirit in 1740 and 1741 when she experienced love, power, and what she called "the sweet nearness of God." Following are excerpts from her husband's *Personal Narrative* in which he quotes Sarah's experiences in her own words:

> On January 28 she wrote: "That night was the sweetest night I ever had in my life. I never before, for so long a time together, enjoyed so much of the light, and rest and sweetness of heaven in my soul ... with a continual, constant and clear sense of Christ's excellent and transcendent love, of His nearness to me, and my dearness to Him, with an inexpressibly sweet calmness of soul in an entire rest in Him...."[38]

The Lord wants you to experience his sweet nearness, the outpouring of his love for you. As he has faithfully come throughout history to those who waited for him, so he will come to you.

[Jesus] told them… "I am going to send you what my Father has promised: but stay in the city until you have been clothed with power from on high."

LUKE 24:46, 49

Come, Holy Spirit, and fill me until I am overflowing with you. I want to experience your power in my life. Give me the gift of your baptism. I wait for you with childlike, expectant faith.

WELCOME HIS SPIRIT

If you are truly born again, it was the Holy Spirit who convicted you of sin, revealed to you the truth of the gospel, and drew you into relationship with Christ. The Holy Spirit is definitely in you from the time of your conversion. But the baptism of the Holy Spirit is subsequent to the salvation experience, as Pastor Jack Hayford explains:

> The Holy Spirit's power must be "received"; it is not an automatic experience. As surely as the Holy Spirit indwells each believer (Romans 8:9), so surely will He fill and overflow each who receives the Holy Spirit in child-like faith (John 7:37-39). When the Holy Spirit fills you, you will know it. Jesus said it and the disciples found it true (Acts 1:4; 2:1-4).[39]

After his resurrection and just before he ascended to heaven, Jesus appeared to his followers and promised that his Father would send them the Holy Spirit. And when the Holy Spirit came they would be "clothed with power." In other words, the Holy Spirit would empower and equip them to fulfill their assignment to carry the gospel message to the ends of the earth. (See Matthew 28:19-20; Acts 1:8.)

Live by the spirit, and you will not gratify the desires of the sinful nature.

GALATIANS 5:16

Hate what is evil; cling to what is good.

ROMANS 12:9

Holy Spirit, fill me this day so that I may think and act in ways that please my Father. Let me hear your still, small voice at every turn, leading me in the way of righteousness.

LIVE EACH DAY IN THE SPIRIT

The Holy Spirit can be described in many ways, but he is repeatedly referred to as a gift. And anyone who accepts Jesus Christ as Savior and asks him for the gift of the Holy Spirit is eligible to receive it.

Well-known author Catherine Marshall, in her book *The Helper*, relates how her experience with the Holy Spirit gradually changed her from the inside out. Shortly after asking God for this gift, she began to be aware of the Spirit's still, small voice in her heart. When she was about to speak harsh or negative words to someone, or even too many words, she would feel a sharp check on the inside. The Holy Spirit began helping her with daily decisions and in her witnessing to others of Jesus.

She writes: "I soon realized that the baptism of the Holy Spirit was no one-time experience, rather a process that would continue throughout my lifetime. True, there was that initial infilling. But how well I knew that I had not thereby been elevated to instant sainthood. In my humanness, self kept creeping back in, so I needed repeated fillings if I were ever to become the mature person God meant me to be."[40]

Then the Lord came down in the cloud and stood there with him [Moses] and proclaimed his name, the Lord. And he passed in front of Moses, proclaiming, "The Lord, the Lord, the compassionate and gracious God, slow to anger, abounding in love and faithfulness." ... When Moses came down from Mount Sinai ... he was not aware that his face was radiant because he had spoken with the Lord."

EXODUS 34:5-6, 29

Father, I welcome your presence into every situation I face today. May all who cross my path experience your love and peace coming through me.

SPEND TIME IN HIS PRESENCE

As we seek God's purpose for our lives, we also need to seek his presence. His *presence* changes us on the inside, but because our bodies are temples of the Holy Spirit, his *power* changes us on the outside. And through us, he can change others.

When Moses came down from Mt. Sinai with the two tables of testimony in his hands, he was unaware that the skin of his face shone, sending forth beams like light—all because he'd been in God's presence.

When we spend time in his presence and allow the Holy Spirit to change us inwardly, our outward behavior and appearance will reflect the result. We can project a sense of peacefulness through our countenance and demeanor that reveals the Holy Spirit's work. Because we are daughters of the King, we actually represent the Lord Jesus everywhere we go.

May God himself, the God of peace, sanctify you through and through. May your whole spirit, soul and body be kept blameless at the coming of our Lord Jesus Christ.

1 THESSALONIANS 5:23

Father, I surrender to you every part of my being. Through the enabling of your Spirit, let my spirit, soul, and body bring honor to you. Let all that is within me be cleansed and strengthened.

LET THE SPIRIT GO DEEP

It's usually the outward, visible things which we tend to concentrate on changing. We know, of course, there's more to life than things we see with our physical eyes, but usually the intangibles are far down on our priority lists.

Scripture teaches that we consist of three parts: spirit, soul, and body. The Holy Spirit wants to work in our lives at each of these three levels, but it must begin with the area of the soul—our mind, emotions, and will. And our will must take the lead. When we *decide* to yield our will to God's will, our thoughts and emotions will follow. This allows the Holy Spirit to reveal—through the spirit part of our being—the areas where attitudes and behaviors need to be changed.

Some believers make the mistake of excusing fleshly sins and weaknesses by claiming that salvation is only for the spirit, not the body. Others go to the opposite extreme, trying through their own strength to attain perfect behavior, feeling they can thus earn their salvation.

Both approaches are wrong. Entering into true Spirit-filled living requires genuine repentance and turning from sin.

I will ask the Father, and he will give you another Counselor to be with you forever—the Spirit of truth.

JOHN 14:16-17a

If you live according to the sinful nature, you will die; but if by the Spirit you put to death the misdeeds of the body, you will live, because those who are led by the Spirit of God are sons [and daughters] of God.

ROMANS 8:13-14

Father, forgive me for resisting the gentle touch of your Spirit. I repent of my willfulness and false confidence in my own strength. I turn from my own way and set my eyes on you.

DON'T NEGLECT THE SPIRIT

How ironic that believers often neglect—through igno-rance, carelessness, pride, or stubbornness—to avail themselves of the help of the Holy Spirit.

God does not force this gift upon his children, and when we do accept his gift, the Holy Spirit is gentle with us. He never overrides our free will.

Author and psychiatrist John White says:

He is willing to show us our helplessness, not only in words but through our experiences. God may do it the slow way, through the normal circumstances of life, or the fast way, by the illumination of the Holy Spirit ... or by a combination of the two.

...We ask him in his own time and way to deal with us, and for the present to take our words seriously. When we do that, God begins to move in on us, whether we perceive it or not. Sooner or later we will begin to see. Sooner or later his own nature begins to be infused with ours.

Curiously, when this happens, you do not become less yourself. That strength and beauty which is uniquely yours, planned from before creation, begins to shine more clearly. You share a family likeness because God is the original source of your being.[41]

Search me, O God, and know my heart; test me and know my anxious thoughts. See if there is any offensive way in me, and lead me in the way everlasting.

PSALM 139:23-24

For it is God who works in you to will and to act according to his good purpose.

PHILIPPIANS 2:13

Lord, I give you permission to spotlight areas where I need to change my behavior or my attitude. I renounce my own willfulness, and choose to cooperate with the Holy Spirit to rid my life of things displeasing to you. I receive your strength.

COOPERATE WITH GOD

To allow the Holy Spirit to guide me and to cooperate with his work of changing me from the inside out requires two things: first, I must acknowledge my own inability to be good enough to earn God's acceptance; second, instead of making excuses for them, I must renounce the areas of weakness and sin which impede my progress toward Spirit-filled living.

We cannot, in our own power, deal a deathblow to all our wrong attitudes and misdeeds. Our innate selfish inclination to yield to fleshly desires is continually at war with Spirit-filled living. When we determine that we truly want to overcome these faults, however, the Holy Spirit strengthens and enables us to begin the process of changing from the inside out. By his power we can experience transformation.

Now the Lord is the Spirit, and where the Spirit of the Lord is, there is freedom. And we, who with unveiled faces all reflect the Lord's glory, are being transformed into his likeness with ever-increasing glory, which comes from the Lord, who is the Spirit.

2 CORINTHIANS 3:17-18

He who began a good work in you will carry it on to completion until the day of Christ Jesus.

PHILIPPIANS 1:6

If anyone is in Christ, he is a new creation; the old has gone; the new has come!

2 CORINTHIANS 5:17

Lord, I can't change myself, but I know that with you all things are possible. Thank you that you are committed to making me more and more like your beloved Son. I say, "Yes!" to your transforming work in my life. Show me moment by moment how to cooperate with you.

SAY "YES" TO YOUR TRANSFORMATION

As women, our natural tendency is to want to change our circumstances, our husband, our children, our home decor, and occasionally our hairstyle. But who wants to change on the inside? Or change our way of thinking? Not many of us volunteer.

To be renewed—or "transformed," as the Scripture says—means to be *changed* by the work of the Holy Spirit. This does not mean change in a cosmetic way, which deals only with the surface, but change in a deep and lasting way which transforms our very nature—in a way which causes us to look at life around us differently.

It is possible for all of us.

The Holy Spirit is the best makeover artist you can imagine, but we have to put ourselves in his hands for his gentle operation. As we yield to the Spirit, we will find some of our most deeply entrenched sin habits giving way so that we may be conformed to the character of Christ.

This time next year, or even a dozen years from now, you will be able to look back and see that you have truly experienced a beautiful metamorphosis.

For you did not receive a spirit that makes you a slave again to fear, but you received the Spirit of sonship. And by him we cry, "Abba, Father." The Spirit himself testifies with our spirit that we are God's children.

ROMANS 8:15-16

I [Paul] pray that out of his glorious riches he may strengthen you with power through his spirit in your inner being, so that Christ may dwell in your hearts through faith.

EPHESIANS 3:16-17

Father, thank you for your incredible Holy Spirit, who can meet my every need. I praise you for doing immeasurably more for me than I could ever ask or imagine.

WHAT AN EXTRAORDINARY GIFT!

The Holy Spirit:

- Confirms our salvation: Rom 8:16; 1 Jn 3:24; 4:13
- Gives life: Rom 8:5-11
- Gives joy: Acts 13:52; Rom 14:17
- Gives hope: Rom 15:13; 1 Thes 1:6
- Liberates: Rom 8:1-2
- Gives strength to overcome sin: Rom 8:9-11; Gal 5:16
- Seals our inheritance in Christ: 1 Cor 1:22; Eph 1:13-14
- Speaks through us: Mt 10:19-20
- Teaches: Lk 12:12; Jn 14:26; 1 Cor 2:13
- Comforts: Jn 14:16 (KJV)
- Testifies of Jesus: Jn 15:26; 1 Jn 5:6
- Convicts of sin: Jn 16:7-8
- Speaks and guides: Jn 16:13; Acts 10:19, 16:6; Rom 8:14
- Empowers to witness: Lk 4:14; Acts 1:8; 1 Pt 1:12
- Enables to speak with tongues: Acts 2:4, 19:6
- Strengthens and encourages: Acts 9:31
- Loves through us: Rom 5:5
- Produces righteous fruit: Gal 5:22-23
- Helps us pray: Rom 8:26-27; 1 Cor 14:15
- Helps us worship: Eph 5:18-19; Phil 3:3
- Reveals the things of God: 1 Cor 2:9-10
- Gives spiritual gifts: 1 Cor 12:7-11
- Edifies our spirits: 1 Cor 14:2,4; Eph 3:16; Jude 1:18-20
- Unites believers: Phil 2:1-2; Eph 4:3-4

What an extraordinary gift the Father bestowed upon his children when he sent the Holy Spirit to be our helper!

PART FOUR:

STANDING FIRM

The tempter came to him and said, "If you are the Son of God, tell these stones to become bread." Jesus answered, "It is written, 'Man does not live on bread alone, but on every word that comes from the mouth of God.'"

MATTHEW 4:3-4

Submit yourselves, then, to God. Resist the devil, and he will flee from you. Come near to God and he will come near to you.

JAMES 4:7-8a

Lord, you see how vulnerable I am to the enemy's schemes when my focus shifts away from you. Help me to gain a greater understanding of your Word and always to resist the enemy and his temptation. I need your strength and wisdom to become a faithful spiritual warrior.

RESIST YOUR ENEMY

Many Christians hold the notion that once they are believers covered by the blood of Jesus, they are immune to the enemy's influence. It is true that Jesus' blood cleanses us from all sin. It is also true that because we belong to him, we have authority over all the power of the enemy. (See Luke 10:19; Ephesians 1:22.) We still have freedom of choice, however. At any time we can choose *not* to obey God and *not* to avail ourselves of the power of the blood of Jesus.

To the degree we choose to walk in our own selfish ways instead of submitting to God, we allow the enemy to gain a foothold in our lives. To the degree we choose to obey—allowing the Holy Spirit to renew our minds through God's Word—we can overcome Satan's efforts to ensnare us! Then we are empowered to battle outwardly, dispelling the powers of darkness and setting other captives free.

The apostle Paul said he disciplined his body so that sins of his flesh would not cause him to lose the inner battle and be disqualified from doing the Lord's work. (See 1 Corinthians 9:26-27.)

Peter took [Jesus] aside and began to rebuke Him, saying, "God forbid it, Lord! This shall never happen to You." But He turned and said to Peter, "Get behind Me, Satan! You are a stumbling block to Me; for you are not setting your mind on God's interests, but man's."

MATTHEW 16:22-23, NASB

Do not conform any longer to the pattern of this world, but be transformed by the renewing of your mind.

ROMANS 12:2

Father, reveal to me any unprotected areas where I've allowed sin to gain a foothold in my life. I want to tear down every idol and submit completely to the renewing power of your Holy Spirit. Help me to live in obedience to your Word. Thank you for your mercy, Lord.

AVOID COMPROMISE

We firmly believe a Christian who is walking in right relationship to God cannot be possessed by a demon. That would imply ownership or total control, and a Christian belongs to Christ, not the devil. But a believer who has compromised with the enemy, who has fallen into idolatry and removed himself from God's protection, can certainly be tormented or harassed or be open to deception by demonic forces. One commentator says:

> Idolatry became not the actual bowing down before a statue but the replacement of God in the mind of the worshiper.... While we may not make or bow down to a statue, we must be constantly on guard that we let nothing come between us and God. As soon as anything does, that thing is an idol.
>
> In addition to material objects such as houses, land, and cars, idols can be people, popular heroes, or those whom we love. Objects of worship can even include things like fame, reputation, hobbies, pride, and deeds done in the name of the Lord. Idolatry is a dangerous and deceitful sin.[42]

Why address this issue? To help women break the cycles of bondage. Then they can move on to fulfill God's purposes for their lives and become effective in spiritual warfare.

My steps have held to your paths; my feet have not slipped.... I have considered my ways and have turned my steps to your statutes. I will hasten and not delay to obey your commands.

PSALM 17:5; 119:59-60

Be sure that you yourself stay away from all sin.

1 TIMOTHY 5:22, LB

Father, increase my sensitivity to what is not pleasing to you. Make me quick to discern these pitfalls and eager to avoid them. I resolve to wait patiently for direction, to learn your ways through studying your Word, and to invite the Spirit to fill me each day.

DISCERN PITFALLS

Here are some common pitfalls that will leave you open to attack from the enemy.

- Deception: Mt 24:4-5, 11, 24-26; 2 Cor 11:3, 14
- Dividing the body of Christ: Eph 4:2-6
- Manipulation: 2 Cor 4:2
- Holding grudges: Eph 4:26-32
- Missing God's timing: Acts 16:6-15
- Unbelief: Heb 3:12-4:2
- Personal ambition; not making room for others' gifts: Phil 2:3-4
- An untamed tongue: Jas 1:26; 3:9-10
- Not obeying the word God gives you: Lk 6:46-49
- Gossip; taking up someone else's offense: 2 Cor 12:20
- Operating out of your mind—not open to the Spirit: 1 Cor 2:12-14
- Lack of vigilance: Eph 6:18; 1 Pt 5:8
- Spiritual pride: 1 Cor 4:18-20
- Dabbling in New Age or other godless philosophies: Col 2:6-8; 2 Tm 4:3-4

The name of the Lord is a strong tower;
the righteous run to it and are safe.

PROVERBS 18:10

No temptation has seized you except what is com-
mon to man. And God is faithful; he will not let you
be tempted beyond what you can bear. But when you
are tempted, he will also provide a way out so that
you can stand up under it.

1 CORINTHIANS 10:13

Thank you, Lord, for being my strong tower in this crisis. I need to know whether this is a test, a temptation, or an attack. Settle my spirit, and help me to receive your discernment as I wait upon you. Lord, I trust you to take me through this situation, and equip me to be more effective in helping others.

TESTING, TEMPTATION, OR ATTACK?

It was Bible teacher Dean Sherman who taught me (Quin) much about the difference between testings, temptations, and the devil's attack. I learned, during a crisis, to ask myself these questions:

- *Is this a test from God?*
- *Is this a temptation?*
- *Is this an attack of the devil?*

Testing develops character, endurance, patience. *Temptation* develops hatred of evil. But an *attack of Satan* makes me learn to depend on the Lord and resist the attack with Scripture. (See James 4:7.)

Is it a test from God? God will test us, just as he tested the children of Israel, but his testing always has a purpose. (See Deuteronomy 8:2, Judges 3:1-4.)

Is it a temptation? Remember, temptation presents the opportunity to sin; it is not sin! When Mrs. Potiphar tried to get the young Joseph into bed with her, he refused. (See Genesis 39:9.)

Is it an attack? If I discern I'm under attack from the devil, I've learned to use Scriptures in spiritual warfare to deflect his onslaught against me or my family.

When Jesus faced the temptation of Satan in the wilderness he was full of the Holy Spirit, and he used the Word of God against the attack. (See Luke 4:1-14.)

Take my yoke upon you and learn from me, for I [Jesus] am gentle and humble in heart, and you will find rest for your souls. For my yoke is easy and my burden is light.

MATTHEW 11:29-30

Be devoted to one another in brotherly love. Honor one another above yourselves. Never be lacking in zeal, but keep your spiritual fervor, serving the Lord.... Live in harmony with one another. Do not be proud, but be willing to associate with people of low position. Do not be conceited.

ROMANS 12:10-11, 16

Father, apart from you I can do nothing. My righteous efforts are but filthy rags. Keep me from boasting except in the work of your Son on my behalf. Give me grace to imitate Jesus' example of humility, giving him glory in all I do.

STAY HUMBLE

Spiritual pride is considering oneself more knowledge-able, more doctrinally correct, or more spiritually gifted than others—the opposite of true humility.

If we heed Paul's warning not to think of ourselves more highly than we ought, the Holy Spirit will protect us from spiritual pride. (See Romans 12:3.) But be aware that the enemy works in subtle ways to ensnare believers with this pitfall. Sometimes spiritual pride masquerades as humility, so we must be sensitive to the Holy Spirit.

Since each of us is made in God's image, we are to show respect for one another, but we must avoid putting certain ones on a pedestal because of their high-profile gifts. Whether in an exalted position or a lowly one, we should keep a biblical perspective of ourselves and of others.

Jesus, knowing who he was, where he had come from, and where he was going, exhibited great humility when he took a towel and washed the disciples' feet. Then he said, "I have set you an example that you should do as I have done for you. I tell you the truth, no servant is greater than his master.... Now that you know these things, you will be blessed if you do them" (John 13:15-17).

David inquired of the Lord, "Shall I go and attack the Philistines?" ... The Lord answered him, "Go, for I will surely hand the Philistines over to you." ... Once more the Philistines came up and spread out in the Valley of Rephaim; so David inquired of the Lord, and he answered, "Do not go straight up, but circle around behind them and attack them in front of the balsam trees."

2 Samuel 5:19, 22-23

If any of you lacks wisdom, he should ask God, who gives generously to all without finding fault, and it will be given to him.

James 1:5

Father, I know you are aware of the circumstances I'm troubled about. I'm asking for your wisdom to know how to fight this battle. Thank you for your promise that you generously give the wisdom we need. I wait upon you, Lord, for clear direction.

SEEK GOD'S STRATEGY

Paul warned the early Christians to stand against the devil's strategies. (See Ephesians 6:11.)

Strategy is the science and art of conducting a military campaign on a broad scale. Tactics are the specific methods you employ to fulfill the strategy plan. A military commander devises a strategy for the overall campaign and the tactics to fulfill it based upon reports from intelligence agents.

If the devil has strategies, then we need God's strategy for the specific battles he calls us to fight. The Holy Spirit is the intelligence agent who knows the enemy's plan. It is critical for us to seek his guidance and fight our battles accordingly.

Linda Raney Wright gives sound advice:

Any activity in terms of spiritual warfare must be done under the leadership of the Holy Spirit. For if God has the last word concerning events that transpire in our lives, then God, alone, can show us what to do, when to do it, and how…. We must totally rely on the leading of the Holy Spirit and the Word of God as to the course we take…. If we are listening and want to follow Him, God will tell us when to fight and when to rest; when to wait and when to move.[43]

Since we have confidence to enter the Most Holy Place by the blood of Jesus, by a new and living way opened for us through the curtain, that is, his body,... let us draw near to God with a sincere heart in full assurance of faith.... Let us hold unswervingly to the hope we profess, for he who promised is faithful.

HEBREWS 10:19-20, 22-23

They overcame him [Satan] by the blood of the Lamb and by the word of their testimony; they did not love their lives so much as to shrink from death.

REVELATION 12:11

Father, nothing is more precious than the blood of Jesus. Thank you for giving your Son as a blood offering for my sin. I rejoice in the blood that paid my debt. May it be on me and those I love to cleanse, guard, and keep us unto the end.

APPLY THE BLOOD

The blood of Jesus, the means of our redemption, is the most precious physical substance ever to touch the earth. In obedience to the law, the Jewish people had for generations offered animal sacrifices to atone for their sins.

When Jesus came to earth, however, he fulfilled the law by becoming the perfect sacrifice, atoning for the sins of all humankind. Abolishing the need for animal sacrifice, his blood is not only precious but powerful.

When we confess our sins and repent of our rebellion against God, we receive forgiveness and cleansing through the blood of Jesus. His blood opens the door to reconciliation with the Father. It delivers us from the curse and power of sin, along with the fear of death. It is also the basis of our authority over the enemy.

To "apply the blood of Jesus" over ourselves and our loved ones in prayer and spiritual warfare is a way of declaring to the devil that Jesus' blood creates a boundary he cannot violate. Only believers who have by faith appropriated Christ's sacrifice for their sins can apply this precious blood.

You can use the power of the blood in spiritual warfare by declaring aloud these scriptures: Exodus 12:13,23; Leviticus 17:11; Hebrews 12:12-14; Romans 5:9-10; Ephesians 1:7-8; Colossians 1:19-20; 2:13-15; Revelation 5:8-10.

For the Lord your God is the one who goes with you to fight for you against your enemies to give you victory.... The Lord will grant that the enemies who rise up against you will be defeated before you. They will come at you from one direction but flee from you in seven.

DEUTERONOMY 20:4; 28:7

"No weapon forged against you will prevail, and you will refute every tongue that accuses you. This is the heritage of the servants of the Lord, and this is their vindication from me," declares the Lord.

ISAIAH 54:17

Father, I look beyond my fears and anxiety over circumstances in my life and the lives of those I love. I look beyond the struggle to the ultimate victory you have already won for us. May this joy set before me sustain me through trials. Lord, help me to remain steadfast until victory comes.

WALK IN VICTORY

Spiritual warriors need to remind themselves and the enemy that his defeat is an irreversible fact. This is best done by wielding the proclamations of God's Word against our adversary, whose ruin is sealed. Arthur Mathews affirms:

Satan is a defeated foe, with a crushed head. There is no power in him, nor are there any means available to him to reach and unseat the Victor of Calvary now seated at the right hand of the Father.

It is not for us to fight *for* victory.... Our fight is *from* victory; and from this vantage point, empowered with Christ's might, and completely enclosed in the whole armor of God, the powers of evil are compelled to back off as we resist them.[44]

Scripture encourages us to look beyond the difficult or seemingly impossible circumstances that Satan often uses to weaken our faith. We must fix our spiritual eyes on Jesus— the author and perfecter of our faith" (Hebrews 12:2)—who secures the victory. By believing God instead of the lies of the enemy, we cooperate with his plan for victory and confound the enemy's plan. Our faith, anchored in God's Word, need not be shaken by circumstances.

One day Jesus was praying in a certain place. When he finished, one of his disciples said to him, "Lord, teach us to pray."

LUKE 11:1

After they had been severely flogged, they were thrown into prison.... About midnight Paul and Silas were praying and singing hymns to God.

ACTS 16:23, 25

Since the day we heard about you, we have not stopped praying for you and asking God to fill you with the knowledge of his will through all spiritual wisdom and understanding.

COLOSSIANS 1:9

Lord, forgive me for the times I've not obeyed the call to prayer. I want to be a faithful prayer warrior. Help me pray according to your will so my prayers will bear fruit for eternity. I make myself available to you for your purposes.

OBEY THE HOLY SPIRIT
IN PRAYER

Very likely you've had the experience of suddenly having a person's name come to mind, or of having a dream about an individual. We suggest you treat such an occurrence as a call from the Holy Spirit to pray for that person or situation. An international prayer minister reminds us of the nature of true prayer:

> Prayer is not our bringing before the Lord all the things that we think are important; prayer is our coming to the point where we are available to listen to what the Lord wants us to deal with in prayer, whatever that might be. If we cannot learn to empty ourselves before God and unwind our busy minds and put down every anxious thought ... we will never come to the place where we will be able to allow the Holy Spirit to begin to inspire us and help us in prayer. The total success of intercessory prayer depends on the source of our intercession— whether the things we are interceding for have been appointed by God, or whether they are of our own choice, our own emotions, or our own burdens.[45]

Then my head will be exalted above the enemies who surround me; at his tabernacle will I sacrifice with shouts of joy; I will sing and make music to the Lord.

PSALM 27:6

Let them praise his name with dancing and make music to him with tambourine and harp. For the Lord takes delight in his people;… May the praise of God be in their mouths and a double-edged sword in their hands.

PSALM 149:3, 4a, 6

Father, free my body, my will, and my emotions to glorify you with my whole life. Make me bolder and less self-conscious. Set my spirit free to worship you. Help me to respond to you at every level of my being.

LEARN HIS WAYS

As you get to know the Lord more intimately and study the Bible, he may highlight by the Spirit things he wants you to do. Things you had never thought of in relation to walking with him—such as:

1. Proclaiming the Word of God around your house or as you walk your neighborhood. (See Jeremiah 3:12; 11:6; Isaiah 55:11; 61:1.)
2. Dancing, either in the privacy of your own home or on a sacred worship team in your church. One woman who uses dance as a way to praise the Lord told us, "When I dance I am worshiping him with my whole body." (See Psalm 149:3-4.)
3. Laughing and shouting for joy. God is restoring laughter to his people. Read the Psalms for many examples of rejoicing in the Lord.
4. Fasting. Times of fasting can yield answers to prayer, direction from God, strategy for warfare, new revelation about Scripture, a closer walk with the Lord, a humbling of self, healing of body, mind, and emotions, and deliverance from evil spirits.
5. Weeping sometimes accompanies deep intercession, either from a spirit of identification or brokenness in the one praying, or during times of intense repentance.

Jehoshaphat appointed men to sing to the Lord and to praise him for the splendor of his holiness as they went out at the head of the army.... As they began to sing and praise, the Lord set ambushes against the men of Ammon and Moab and Mount Seir who were invading Judah, and they were defeated.

2 CHRONICLES 20:21, 22

Through Jesus, therefore, let us continually offer to God a sacrifice of praise—the fruit of lips that confess his name.

HEBREWS 13:15

Father, you deserve all glory, honor, and power forever and ever! You are perfect in all your ways and kind in all your deeds, and your love endures forever. You are worthy of my praise and I worship you. There is none like you!

PRAISE

Praise. Adulation. Commendation. We heap such sentiments on people after they achieve a goal or perform in some way, but keen spiritual warriors learn the power of praising God *before* seeing evidence of his intervention in the prayer concern. We can offer thanksgiving with such confidence because of who he is: a God of love, faithfulness, holiness, and justice.

Scripture declares, "He is the Rock, his works are perfect, and all his ways are just. A faithful God who does no wrong, upright and just is he" (Deuteronomy 32:4). When we praise God despite negative circumstances, we affirm his power and victory over those circumstances.

A.W. Tozer wrote, "True Christian joy is the heart's harmonious response to the Lord's song of love."[46] That harmonious response bursts forth in praise. Three important results flow from our praise:

1. God receives glory.
2. Our faith is increased, and we are energized by the joy of the Lord that accompanies praise.
3. The enemy is terrified and his plans confounded.

Since the devil knows the power of praise, he works diligently to discourage Christians from using this potent weapon against his dark kingdom.

Those who sow in tears will reap with songs of joy.
He who goes out weeping, carrying seed to sow, will
return with songs of joy, carrying sheaves with him.

PSALM 126:5-6

Rend your heart and not your garments. Return to
the Lord your God, for he is gracious and compas-
sionate, slow to anger and abounding in love, and he
relents from sending calamity.... Let the priests, who
minister before the Lord, weep between the temple
porch and the altar. Let them say, "Spare your people,
O Lord. Do not make your inheritance an object of
scorn, a byword among the nations."

JOEL 2:13, 17

Lord, you see my tears as I identify with the hurting, lost
ones for whom I intercede. Give me a heart of compassion.
Help me to be able to pray with discernment and wisdom
for the ones you put on my heart. Please receive my tears
as intercession for their deepest needs.

WEEP

Dick Eastman, popular teacher on prayer and intercession, comments on Psalm 126:

Tears in Scripture play a unique role in spiritual breakthrough. Here we discover that the planting of seeds accompanied by a spirit of brokenness will not only bring a spiritual harvest of results, but will leave the sower with a spirit of rejoicing in the process. This passage, along with numerous others in Scripture regarding a spirit of brokenness, pictures a variety of purposes and functions related to what might be termed "the ministry of tears," a ministry Charles H. Spurgeon defined as "liquid prayer."

Eastman goes on to mention six different types of tears:

1. Tears of sorrow or suffering. (See 2 Kings 20:5.)
2. Tears of joy. (See Genesis 33:4.)
3. Tears of compassion. (See John 11:35.)
4. Tears of desperation. (See Esther 4:1, 3.)
5. Tears of travail. (See Isaiah 42:14.)
6. Tears of repentance. (See Joel 2:12-13.)[47]

In our quiet times with the Lord, we may find ourselves weeping or in travail as we pray due to any of the above reasons. The psalmist David once prayed, "Record my lament; list my tears on your scroll—are they not in your record? Then my enemies will turn back when I call for help. By this I will know that God is for me" (Psalm 56:8-9).

"For if you remain silent at this time, relief and deliverance for the Jews will arise from another place, but you and your father's family will perish. And who knows but that you have come to royal position for such a time as this?" Then Esther sent this reply to Mordecai: "... I and my maids will fast as you do. When this is done, I will go to the king,... And if I perish, I perish."

ESTHER 4:14-16

Is not this the kind of fasting I have chosen: to loose the chains of injustice and untie the cords of the yoke, to set the oppressed free and break every yoke?... Then you will call, and the Lord will answer; you will cry for help, and he will say: Here am I.

ISAIAH 58:6, 9

Father, may I learn balance and discipline in all that I undertake, just as Esther did. May I pray and seek your face, taking action only after I know your will. Give me courage and purpose so that I will be useful to you when you call me to a task.

FAST AND PRAY

Queen Esther is a biblical example of how strong a woman can be. When facing a crisis that threatened the annihilation of the Jews, she called for a period of fasting and prayer before she took action on her own. Then she put her life on the line by going to the king and intervening for her people's lives.

Perhaps the greatest lessons we can learn from Esther are *discipline* and *balance*. She did not rush to implement a plan of her own without seeking God's direction, nor did she take a passive role and say, "If God wants to do something, he can do it." Disciplining herself and her people through a fast, she balanced that by taking action one step at a time.

Esther's story provides an excellent model for fighting our own tough spiritual battles. We see her following three important principles:

1. She settled in her heart that this battle was one in which she should be involved. She was in the palace "for such a time as this," and her commitment was solid.
2. She called the Jewish people to a fast, recognizing a solution was beyond her human wisdom. She would have to rely totally upon God.
3. She took action one step at a time, expecting God's direction at each juncture.

When you fast, do not look somber as the hypocrites do, for they disfigure their faces to show men they are fasting. I tell you the truth, they have received their reward in full. But when you fast, put oil on your head and wash your face; so that it will not be obvious to men that you are fasting, but only to your Father who is unseen; and your Father, who sees what is done in secret, will reward you.

MATTHEW 6:16-18

Father, lead me beyond my flesh and deeper into the things of the Spirit. Help me to discipline my flesh through fasting so that I might develop spiritual strength to accomplish more for your kingdom.

MASTER YOUR APPETITES

D*ake's Annotated Reference Bible* offers the view that fasting is the antidote for unbelief:

> The disciples asked the Lord why they could not heal a lunatic boy. Jesus said, "Because of your unbelief ... Howbeit this kind goeth not out but by prayer and fasting" (Matthew 17:20, 21, KJV). Faith needs prayer for its development and full growth, and prayer needs fasting for the same reason.... To fast means to abstain from food—that which caused the fall of man.
>
> Fasting humbles the soul before God, chastens the soul, and crucifies the appetites and denies them so as to give time to prayer. It manifests earnestness before God to the exclusion of all else, shows obedience, gives the digestive system a rest, demonstrates the mastery of man over appetites, aids in temptation, helps to attain power over demons, develops faith, crucifies unbelief, and aids in prayer.[48]

Some Christians are reluctant to fast because they fear it can lead to fanaticism or occultism. We are aware that fasting is practiced by spiritists and adherents of false religions to sharpen their sensitivities to the spiritual realm and to invite demons to give them power. But Jesus spoke of fasting at the same time he taught his followers how to pray and how to give. All three are disciplines the Christian should observe.

"The God of heaven will give us success. We his servants will start rebuilding, but as for you [Sanballat and enemies], you have no share in Jerusalem, or any claim or historic right to it...."

I stood up and said to the nobles, the officials and the rest of the people, "Don't be afraid of them. Remember the Lord, who is great and awesome, and fight for your brothers, your sons and your daughters, your wives and your homes."

NEHEMIAH 2:20, 4:14

When the storm has swept by, the wicked are gone, but the righteous stand firm forever.

PROVERBS 10:25

I praise you, Lord, that I do not have to be afraid when the enemy comes to assault me or my family. You are a great and awesome God, and I trust you to turn back from us the insults of the enemy—just as you did for Nehemiah. Thank you for your faithfulness.

STAND AGAINST THE ENEMY

When I (Quin) need a pattern for battle, I study again the book of Nehemiah. An exiled Jew in Babylon, Nehemiah was cupbearer to the king of Persia when he learned the walls of Jerusalem lay in ruins. He wept, mourned, fasted, and prayed because of the condition of his homeland.

Then when the time was right, Nehemiah got the king's permission to go to Jerusalem and start the project. First he scouted out the land. Then calling the elders together, he shared his plan, and they pledged their cooperation.

Nehemiah's foe was Sanballat, who with his companions taunted the Israelites, mocking and ridiculing them. But Nehemiah talked back to the enemy. In like manner, we must declare to the enemy that we are taking back the territory he has claimed in our family. He has no legal or historic right to it.

Nehemiah also asked God to cause the enemy's plan against him and his countrymen to backfire. Using his prayer as an example, we can ask God to let the devil's plan of attack against our family turn and bring damage to his own camp. (See Nehemiah 4:4-5.) We can remind Satan that his tactic against Jesus resulted in his own defeat.

Let the righteous rejoice in the Lord and take refuge in him; let all the upright in heart praise him!

PSALM 64:10

When the Lord brought back the captives to Zion, we were like men who dreamed. Our mouths were filled with laughter, our tongues with songs of joy. Then it was said among the nations, "The Lord has done great things for them." The Lord has done great things for us, and we are filled with joy.

PSALM 126:1-3

Rejoice in the Lord always. I will say it again: Rejoice!

PHILIPPIANS 4:4

Father, I long to laugh and shout for joy, but often I am so mired in the burden of the battle that I lose perspective. Restore to me the joy of your salvation. Thank you that I can find my hope and my joy in you.

REJOICE

Psalm 126 tells us how the Jews expressed their joy when they returned from Babylonian captivity after seventy years. They had a grand celebration when the work of rebuilding the wall was completed. The people wept, sang, bowed down, and celebrated as Nehemiah reminded them, "Do not grieve, for the joy of the Lord is your strength" (Nehemiah 8:10).

In the Bible, women who rejoiced include Miriam, Hannah, and Mary. King David gave praise to God seven times a day. Daniel, who prayed three times a day while he was in captivity, also gave thanks. One of the most liberating things you can do—even before your victory is complete—is to walk in praise, rejoicing, and laughter.

Many biblical references to laughter mean "to mock, to make sport, to deride, to laugh, to scorn." Scripture records that God laughs at the enemy: "The wicked plot against the righteous and gnash their teeth at them; but the Lord laughs at the wicked, for he knows their day is coming" (Psalm 37:12-13).

Let's continue to stand as unyielding intercessors, rebuilding broken, burned walls that have given the enemy access. You can laugh, sing, or shout your way to victory!

NOTES

1. R. Arthur Mathews, *Born for Battle* (Robesonia, Pa.: OMF Books, 1978), 31–32.
2. C.S. Lewis, *The Screwtape Letters* (New York: Macmillan, 1961), 3.
3. William Gurnall, *The Christian in Complete Armour*, Vol. 1, abridged by Ruthanne Garlock, et al. (Carlisle, Pa.: Banner of Truth Trust, 1986), 54.
4. Gurnall, Vol. 1, 66, 68.
5. W.E. Vine, *Vine's Expository Dictionary of Old and New Testament Words*, Vol. 3 (Old Tappan, N.J.: Fleming H. Revell, 1981), 298–99.
6. Gurnall, Vol. 1, 29.
7. Gurnall, Vol. 2, 149, 160.
8. Gurnall, Vol. 2, 386, 388.
9. Gurnall, Vol. 3, 27, 28, 30, 31.
10. Dean Sherman, *Spiritual Warfare for Every Christian* (Seattle: Frontline Communications, 1990), 45.
11. Roger C. Palms, *Bible Readings on Hope* (Minneapolis: Worldwide Publications, 1995), 49.
12. Mathews, 17, 54.
13. Mathews, 22.
14. Paul E. Billheimer, *Destined to Overcome* (Minneapolis: Bethany House, 1982), 41, 43.
15. David Wilkerson, "What It Means to Walk in the Spirit," *Times Square Church Pulpit Series*, August 15, 1994, 1.
16. Elizabeth Alves, *The Mighty Warrior: A Guide to Effective Prayer* (Bulverde, Tex.: Intercessors International, 1992), 74–77.
17. Sherman, 42, 43.
18. Ted Haggard, "A Pastor's Prayer Principles," *Ministries Today* (Lake Mary, Fla.: Strang Communications, November–December, 1994), 17.
19. Corrie ten Boom, *Marching Orders for the End Battle* (Fort Washington, Pa.: Christian Literature Crusade, 1969), 33–34.
20. Jack Hayford, *Prayer is Invading the Impossible* (New York: Ballantine, 1983), 49–51. (Copyright by Logos, International, 1977; used with permission of the author.)
21. Hannah Whitall Smith, *The God of All Comfort* (Chicago: Moody, 1956), 112.
22. Ruth Myers, *31 Days of Praise* (Sisters, Ore.: Multnomah, 1994), 127.
23. A.W. Tozer, *The Best of A.W. Tozer* compiled by Warren W. Wiersbe (Harrisburg, Pa.: Christian Publications, 1978), 121–22.
24. Sherman, 107.

25. H. Norman Wright, *Always Daddy's Girl* (Ventura, Calif.: Regal, 1989), 235–36.

26. Nancy Clarke, *Connection* (newsletter of Women's Aglow Fellowship International, Edmonds, Wash.), December 1990, 6.

27. Dr. Archibald Hart, *Healing Life's Hidden Addictions* (Ann Arbor, Mich.: Servant, 1990), 164.

28. Richard J. Foster, *The Challenge of the Disciplined Life* (San Francisco: Harper & Row, 1985), 204.

29. Gordon D. Fee, *God's Empowering Presence* (Peabody, Mass.: Hendrickson, 1994), 449–50.

30. Eileen Wallis, *Queen Take Your Throne* (Columbia, Mo.: Cityhill, 1987), 61–62.

31. Notes on Galatians 5:22. *The Spirit-Filled Life Bible*, ed. Jack Hayford (Nashville, Tenn.: Thomas Nelson, 1991), 1780.

32. Fee, 450–51.

33. Fee, 451.

34. William Barclay, *The Letters to the Galatians and Ephesians* (Philadelphia: Westminster, 1976), 51, 52.

35. *Strong's Exhaustive Concordance of the Bible*, Greek reference #2904, and *The Reader's Digest Illustrated Dictionary and Concordance of the Bible* (Reader's Digest Association, 1992), 1219.

36. Herbert Lockyer, *All About the Holy Spirit* (Peabody, Mass.: Hendrickson, 1995), 106, 107.

37. Donald Lee Barnett & Jeffrey P. McGregor, *Speaking in Other Tongues: A Scholarly Defense* (Seattle: Community Chapel, 1986), Chapter 5, Part V, 228–54.

38. Guy Chevreau, *Catch the Fire* (Toronto, Canada: Harper Collins, 1995), 78, 79, 82-83.

39. Jack Hayford, "Kingdom Dynamics," *The Spirit-Filled Life Bible,* 1622.

40. Catherine Marshall, *The Helper* (Grand Rapids, Mich.: Baker, 1988), 66–67.

41. John White, *Changing on the Inside* (Ann Arbor, Mich.: Servant, 1991), 156.

42. Herbert Lockyer, Sr., ed., *Nelson's Illustrated Bible Dictionary* (Nashville, Tenn.: Thomas Nelson, 1986), 501.

43. Linda Raney Wright, *Spiritual Warfare and Evangelism,* (Crestline, Calif.: Linda Raney Wright), 9.

44. Mathews, 26–28.

45. Johannes Facius, *Explaining Intercession* (Tonbridge, Kent, England: Sovereign World Ltd., 1993), 39–40.

46. A.W. Tozer, *The Knowledge of the Holy* (San Francisco: Harper & Row, 1964), 102.

47. Dick Eastman, "Advancing in Spiritual Warfare," *The Spirit-Filled Life Bible,* 865.

48. Finis Jennings Dake, *Dake's Annotated Reference Bible* (Lawrenceville, Ga.: Dake Bible Sales, 1963), 629.